365

Prescriptions

for the

Soul

365

Prescriptions
for the
Soul

Daily Messages of
Inspiration, Hope, and Love

DR. BERNIE S. SIEGEL

NEW WORLD LIBRARY
NOVATO, CALIFORNIA

New World Library
14 Pamaron Way
Novato, California 94949

Copyright © 2004 by Bernie S. Siegel

Edited by Andrea Hurst
Cover design and typography by Cathey Flickinger

Library of Congress Cataloging-in-Publication Data
Siegel, Bernie S.
365 prescriptions for the soul : daily messages of inspiration, hope, and love /
Bernie S. Siegel.
p.   cm.
ISBN 1-57731-425-5 (hardcover : alk. paper)
1. Meditations. 2. Spiritual life. I. Title.
BL624.2.S56   2004
204'.32—dc22   2003 017742

First Printing, December 2003
ISBN 1-57731-425-5
Printed in Canada on acid-free, partially recycled paper
Distributed to the trade by Publishers Group West

10 9 8 7 6 5 4 3 2 1

SPECIAL THANKS

I want to thank God.
I would also like to extend a very special thanks to Andrea Hurst and her associates for their patience and assistance.

I DEDICATE THIS BOOK

*to my soulmates and teachers in this life
and in past lives. I am sure they will continue
to enlighten me in future lives until I get it right:*

*My parents: Rose and Simon Siegel
My wife: Barbara (Bobbie) Siegel
Our children: Jonathan, Jeffrey, Stephen,
Carolyn, and Keith
Their spouses: Judy, Marcia, Roy, and Jane
Our grandchildren: Charles, Samuel, Gabriel,
Elijah, Simone, Jarrod, Patrick, and Jason*

*Bless you all for what you do for me,
and may I someday live up to what you all deserve
in a son, husband, and father.*

*Desire and intention are the most dynamic
of our faculties; they do work. They are the
true explorers of the infinite, the instruments
of our ascent to God. Reason comes
to the foot of the mountain; it is the
industrious will urged by the passionate
heart which climbs the slope.*

— EVELYN UNDERHILL

Introduction

I wrote *365 Prescriptions for the Soul* to provide the reader with a daily guide and resource for navigating the troubled waters and challenges of life. This book is an accumulation of my life experiences and the knowledge I've gleaned from studying the wisdom of the sages. My most significant insights have been gained through my work with patients diagnosed with life-threatening or disabling illnesses. Their wisdom and teachings have profoundly changed my life for the better, and I hope they will do the same for you.

The prescriptions contained in this book are bite-sized bits of wisdom presented in a manner that is accessible and fits easily into our busy lives. Each daily entry guides you peacefully, lovingly, and consciously through life's challenges, preparing you for whatever may come your way. In today's mechanized, technology-based society, we are often informed but rarely truly educated. We absorb an enormous amount of information from the various media — television, radio, newspapers, and the Internet — but does any of this information truly prepare or inspire us? Everybody faces obstacles in life; those who succeed in getting past them learn something in the process. I can still hear my father telling me that one of the best things that happened to him, when he was twelve, was his father dying. It taught him what was important about life and to be kind to other people. Sometimes it takes a disaster to wake us up and make us realize the blessings we have.

Ernest Hemingway said, "The world breaks everyone, and afterward, some become strong at the broken places." As a physician I can tell you that Hemingway was right about bone fractures. But why wait until we break down or fall apart to learn this truth in our spiritual and emotional lives? Why not acquire the tools and insights to prevent fracturing under trying conditions by becoming strong enough to deal with life and learning how to bend?

Too often it takes a direct confrontation with one's mortality to learn the value of the limited time we all have on earth. Many of us believe that time is money. Time isn't money; time is everything. The way we spend our time is what our life is all about. If we spend our time paying attention to the wisdom of our heart rather than the wisdom of our head, we will benefit greatly.

So why not follow this "doctor's orders"? My prescription for you is to use this book as part of your daily ritual. Take the time to read a selection and reflect on its meaning for you. Allow it to make a difference in your day, and help heal your life and the lives of those you touch. May this book guide you to a place where your heart will find true peace.

Doctor's Orders

THE SYMBOL Rx means "dispense as written." Sometimes a prescription can be very helpful. But information alone does not lead one to change unless it is combined with inspiration.

You will not fill a prescription or let it help you, unless you choose to *follow its directions*. The prescriptions I ask you to fill are designed for your total well-being. They come from hard-earned wisdom and experience with the difficulties of life. They will help you to develop healthy self-love, self-esteem, and self-worth and to heal the wounds of the past. My hope is they will help you to find true meaning in your life.

Introduction

If you are in a great deal of pain or acutely ill you may want to take one "Q4HPRN," meaning every four hours as necessary. You may also try different prescriptions to find what works best for you. You cannot overdose during difficult times, and there are no adverse side effects. However, when stable, I suggest using the Rx "TID" or "QID," which means three or four times a day so that you restore yourself and give your body a "live" message throughout the day and at bedtime.

You will feel and sleep better if you fill your prescriptions and use them regularly.

Peace,
Bernie S. Siegel, M.D.

SOULUTIONS

When the soul collects all its interior powers within, and when the body collects all its external senses and unites them to the soul, the Holy Spirit approaches and breathes into this union quietude and peace.

— FATHER ANDREW LEONARD
WINCZEWSKI, O.S.B.

WHAT IS A SOULUTION? First let me define *solution*. A solution comes from our intellect. It is an attempt to solve a difficulty or dilemma by figuring out what the right thing to do is in any problematic circumstance. It comes from the mind and is based on thinking.

A *soul*ution helps you to solve your problems by taking a broad approach. It speaks to you through your feelings, dreams, and visions and not through words alone. A soulution leads to right action. It truly resolves conflicts and difficulties in ways that lead to a deeper sense of peace.

Soulution of the Day

Accept the wisdom of your soul. Listen to the words it speaks, observe the dreams and visions it creates, and respond to your soulful feelings. Read on and pay particular attention to the Soulutions offered in this book.

SLOW DOWN

*There is more to life
than increasing its speed.*

— MOHANDAS GANDHI

MY WIFE IS ALWAYS TELLING ME to slow down, but my years of medical training have taught me to do things quickly to be prepared for emergencies. Although it's been hard to stop walking fast and gulping down meals, I keep trying!

The other day a policeman waved at me to slow down as I passed a construction site, and this led me to think about my wife's message.

Then, a few days later as I left my office and started walking toward my car, I heard a woman say, "Slow down!" So I did. As I started to walk slowly, I heard another woman start laughing. I turned to see what was funny, and it was *me*. She pointed out that the person saying "Slow down" was the mother of a little boy who had run into the parking lot as they left the building. I said, "Now you know what my wife and mother have been telling me for years. So I follow orders when I hear a woman's voice say 'slow down!'"

Sometimes the Creator works in mysterious ways. If the same message is coming to you from many different directions, heed it!

Soulution of the Day

*As the Sufi poet Rumi says, "Your criticism polishes my mirror."
When we hear the same suggestions over and over again,
they may begin to feel like criticism. But if you stop to listen,
they might just help you to slow down and smell the roses.*

GREATEST TRUTH

*Love has no other desire
but to fulfill itself.*

— KAHLIL GIBRAN

THE GREATEST TRUTH I know about life is that love is the answer. If you ask me what the question is, I will tell you it is every question you could ever ask. Love is always the answer to every question and problem. We are here to love and be loved and learn a few things in the process.

I can never be wrong when I choose to love. Love rewards me by bringing meaning to my life. I know when I choose to love I will always be in the right place at the right time. It provides my life with the order and harmony that bring me peace.

All I ask of life is to be given the chance to love, and I pray that I will be able to do that, despite my imperfections. My days are devoted to acting as if I am the lover I want to be, and I know someday I will become who I hope to be. Until that day, those around me remain grateful for my attempt.

Soulution of the Day

Whatever your problem is, the solution is love.

ACCEPTANCE

God grant me the serenity to accept the things I cannot change, the courage to change the things I can, and the wisdom to know the difference.

— THE SERENITY PRAYER

WHAT IS TRULY LASTING? Polar ice melts. The ozone layer shrinks. A relationship ends. Your family or friends act differently for no apparent reason. So what can you rely on? There is only one thing — change. Change is the one constant that is ever present.

On a personal level, you do have choices about how you change. But the rest of the universe is not under your control. All of the universes, including ours, are like portions of God's canvas. They are constantly being worked and reworked. The Creator must have his or her reasons, and hopefully we will understand them someday.

Understanding won't eliminate change. But acceptance of this truth will enable us to live in a more peaceful state. When we don't resist change, we flow with the process of creation and help make it a true work of art.

Soulution of the Day

Say the Serenity Prayer when feeling troubled, and remember its message.

BEGINNINGS

*To begin anew, we must say good-bye
to who we once were.*

— ANONYMOUS

THE FIRST TIME I was asked to give a report to the Board of Directors of Heaven I was quite nervous. When I finished I said, "The end," and God said, "No, that's not the end."

I thought I was in big trouble because I hadn't done a good job, so I said, "That's the end of my report. I have no more to say."

God responded, "I understand, but in Heaven when we finish a report we say, The Beginning. For instance, does the Bible end in conclusions?"

"No, Revelations," I said.

"Right," God said. "And do you call a graduation a termination?"

"No, it's a commencement."

"Right again. Remember, Bernie, life is a series of beginnings. The changes, losses, illnesses, and afflictions are not endings, but beginnings. We are changed and have to start a new life each time. So what do you say now?"

"I shall try to find for myself, my family, and my patients the strength and courage to live this way."

The meeting was adjourned.

Soulution of the Day

*Have the courage to begin the new life that each day brings you.
No matter what changes or losses you have experienced,
step back and see where you need to begin.*

JOY

And Joy is Everywhere;
It is in the Earth's green covering of grass;
In the blue serenity of the Sky.

— RABINDRANATH TAGORE, *JOY*

HOW DO WE FIND JOY IN OUR LIVES? Too often it comes at a significant price. You learn you are mortal, and suddenly what used to seem important isn't. Things that used to bother you don't anymore because they have become insignificant. What then becomes significant are the people who you love and who love you.

When you know your time is limited, every moment becomes precious. You step out the door, and a flower brings you joy because it may be the last flower you ever see. Time becomes a gift, not a burden, because you choose to spend it with the things and people you love and stop doing the things that are meaningless. You wear whatever you like and stop worrying so much about what others think. When you appreciate the now, weather becomes fascinating instead of a problem. It turns a frost-covered window blocking your vision into an awesome work of art.

Enjoy what lies before you, and be in awe of the beauty of creation. What I have learned from the words, "Seeing something for the last time is almost as good as the first" is to start seeing everything for the first time again. I think of myself as an extraterrestrial every morning and see the world as if it were my first day on earth.

Soulution of the Day

Today try being an extraterrestrial and glory in the beauty
and variety before you.

WE ARE LIKE TWO BIRDS

Love conquers all things;
Let us surrender to love.

— VIRGIL

THE OTHER DAY I WATCHED TWO GEESE FLYING BY. The male was leading and honking to his mate, who followed behind him and reassured him with her answering honks. They are a unit and experience life together. Their fidelity makes the pains of life tolerable for them both and brings them more joy.

They reminded me of when my wife and I go out biking. I lead or follow to make it safer for her and ring my bell when I am concerned about where she is riding. When we open our hearts to others and allow them into our lives, our journey becomes meaningful.

I once wrote a poem for my wife entitled "A Beautiful Burden." In it I speak about all the traveling, especially flying, that we do together. I always carry all of the luggage, and tease my wife about how heavy hers is and how love is supposed to make one's burdens lighter! She knows that her presence brightens my day and makes all the traveling more joyful. To quote the last lines of my poem:

> *I learned from traveling alone*
> *That the load is really no lighter*
> *For a lonely heart weighs more*
> *Than a bag that can't be packed any tighter.*

Soulution of the Day

The birdcalls and the call of one's mate are the call to life.

FOOTSTEPS

Sometimes what looks like fresh footprints that will lead you to a new destination is really only a sign of a well-beaten path.

— LIN ANN HO

ONE DAY AFTER A BIG SNOWSTORM I was jogging through the deep snow and really struggling to make my way. I realized how much of an effort it was to make my way with no plowed path or footsteps to follow. The next day it was much easier. The snow was still soft, and my footprints were easy to follow. Five days later the snow had frozen, and the rigid ice made it dangerous for me to try to fit into the old footprints. I had to create a new path or risk breaking my ankles.

What I learned is that at different times in my life I must make different choices. At times it is all right to be carried. At other times, following in the footsteps of others is appropriate, and at others you must make your own way. Sometimes it is proper to leave the old ways and start a fresh path. You find your way by attending to what feels right for you and not by looking for the easy way.

You must remember that if you constantly follow in the steps of others you will lose your way. Remember that at times other people's ways may be wrong for you and even endanger you. So find your own way and let others go theirs. True natives can be your guides only when they have shared your experience.

Soulution of the Day

Make your own path. Do not follow those who are not true guides, for if you do, you may be lost forever.

PASSWORDS

Passwords are the words that help you pass through the strange and bad lands of life's experience.

— BEN ZION

MANY WORDS AND SAYINGS stay with us as we go through life. I call them "passwords." When I run into difficulties I recall words that help me deal with whatever is before me. A whole book may be a password if it teaches me how to handle something the author has already overcome.

Sometimes it is one word that when repeated, like a mantra, sustains me. Or it may be an Internet password that leads me to helpful information. We all need to find the passwords that get us through, just as a passport gets us through customs when entering a different country.

My favorite passwords are *love, laughter, faith, prayer,* and *miracle.* I use *miracle* more than any other because it keeps me open and expecting the positive aspects of life. For me, it's a reminder of what Dr. Carl Simonton said: "In the face of uncertainty there is nothing wrong with hope."

Soulution of the Day

Pass your words of hope on to others.

OH, MY GOD!

I cannot prove to you that God exists, but my work has proved empirically that the pattern of God exists in every man and that this pattern in the individual has at its disposal the greatest transforming energies of which life is capable. Find this pattern in your own individual self and life is transformed.

— C. G. JUNG

OH, MY GOD! When you see those words, what do you think? Many of us use the word "God" without any clear concept of what we are talking about. Stop and ask yourself what God means to you. If you had to write an essay on God, what would you say about him, her, it? You see how easy it is to get into problems trying to describe God. Words don't fit, and that's the problem. Some say, "God is love." But they don't define love, and love has no gender associated with it. I don't see my God as having a gender or human form.

If I had to describe my God I'd say, "Look around you and you'll see my God. My God is in you and the tree and the computer. My God has many faces, and we are all one of them. God is love and more. God is things we can't touch, like consciousness, intelligence, and energy, and God is things we can touch like matter and the things that matter. We are all God, or at least an extension of God."

Soulution of the Day

Contemplate what God means to you.

HORSE SENSE

The outside of a horse does good for the inside of a man.

— WINSTON CHURCHILL

ONE DAY I FOUND A HORSE roaming free near our home. I jumped on him and got him back on the road. Whenever he strayed from the road, I guided him back. Many miles from where we started he turned into a farm. The farmer said, "That's my horse. How did you know he belonged here?"

"I didn't know," I replied. "The horse knew. All I did was keep him on the road."

The horse has an intuitive wisdom and follows it.

Another time I tried to keep a horse I was riding from going under a tree. I stood up in the saddle and pulled with all my might on the reins, but the horse won and a branch of the tree knocked me out of the saddle. The horse left and I waited. I knew he would go back to the barn and that people would come looking for me.

Sometimes we have guides and teachers that help keep us on the path. At other times people and events lead us astray. But ultimately we all need to live like the horse and know our own way home.

Soulution of the Day

Where is your home? If you were a horse, and someone let go of your reins, where would you head?

BLACK HOLES OF RENEWAL

*The cave you fear to enter
holds the treasure you seek.*

— JOSEPH CAMPBELL

WHEN WE NEED to find our energy and source, the place to look is in the darkness. It is in the black holes that the energy of creation lives. Whether we are speaking of the universe or of an individual, darkness is the source of life.

When facing emotional despair, hopelessness, or physical anguish, going into the darkness helps us to find our self and renew our life. It is in the nothingness that we can stop and find peace and answers. When we see our true potential, we can then create ourselves anew. We can become like a blank canvas and begin the act of creation out of the darkness.

When I lecture, I hold up a piece of paper with a black dot on it and then ask people to describe what they see. Many say a black dot, while others answer correctly and say a piece of paper with a dot on it. You can decide to focus on the darkness or use it to appreciate that your life contains light too. You would never appreciate the light if you didn't have the darkness.

Don't be afraid of the darkness. Let the Director show you the way! Go inside, discover your own black hole, and emerge with new energy and the true light of awareness. Let the tomb become a womb.

Soulution of the Day

Spend some time in the dark today.

SUPERSTITION

*Be strong, get beyond all superstitions,
and be free.*

— SWAMI VIVEKANANDA

SOME FEARS ARE JUST SUPERSTITIONS. For instance, why fear the number thirteen? In Judaism a boy or girl's thirteenth birthday is a day to celebrate and have a bar or bat mitzvah.

So what is superstition? Many of us still hold to superstitions in our daily lives, such as when we avoid walking under a ladder or when we worry about a black cat crossing our path. The dictionary says: **superstition** 1. A belief or notion not based on reason or knowledge, in or of the significance of a particular thing, circumstance, occurrence, proceeding, or the like. 2. A system or collection of such beliefs. 3. A custom or act based on such beliefs.

There are enough real fears in life; we do not need to add to them by bringing in what are really just superstitions.

Soulution of the Day

How often do you let superstition run your life?

LAUGHTER

Laughter is the most healthful exertion.

— CHRISTOPH WILHELM HUFELAND

LAUGHTER IS an external manifestation of an internal gift. When you laugh, you are changing your internal chemistry and creating a healthy environment in you so that healing can occur. Norman Cousins wrote about his experience with laughter and healing, and his conclusion was that our beliefs are our biology.

My way of saying it is your feelings are your chemistry. Laughter not only produces pleasant feelings and images for you and others, but it also alters your body chemistry. Can you laugh yourself into wellness? It is possible. When you spend your life smiling at the world, you will live a longer, healthier life.

Years ago during a difficult period as a young physician, unaware of how to deal with my feelings, I kept a journal of my day's experiences. This journal was filled with pain, and I kept it hidden. One night I forgot to put it away, and my wife, Bobbie, found it. She said, "Honey, there is nothing funny in it." I replied, "My life isn't funny."

She then reminded me of all the funny things I had told her about that I had not included in my journal...like the time a capped, masked, and gowned man walked into my patient's room. The patient was in isolation and started to get undressed, thinking he was there to examine her. After watching her for a minute or two he said, "You don't have to do that for me; I'm here to mop the floor." Afterward they became very good friends. After my talk with Bobbie, I included the humorous things that had happened to me as well as the difficult ones in my journal. It was a much more fulfilling experience that way.

Soulution of the Day

Choose to find things to laugh about. You will change, and so will all the people you meet. You will not burn out when you can laugh at life.

PRESCRIPTION #15

ATTITUDE

I am convinced that life is 10 percent what happens to you and 90 percent how you react to it. And so it is with you.

— CHARLES SWINDOLL

STUDIES SHOW that optimists live longer, healthier lives than pessimists, even when the pessimist's view of life is more accurate. We could go on with endless quotes of famous people talking about all the things they worried about that never happened.

My friend Dr. Karl Menninger said, "Attitudes are more important than facts." That is why what we tell ourselves is extremely significant and helps to shape our destiny. If our self-talk gives us hope and a positive outlook, we will live very different lives than if we await trouble and think that bad things always follow the good.

You know the old saying "What you see is what you get." Your attitude determines what you see, so always look on the bright side. The choice is yours.

Soulution of the Day

*See through the eyes of an optimist today
and observe what direction your life takes.*

MIRROR, MIRROR

Just as we cannot see our own faces without looking into a mirror, we cannot know ourselves without looking into our soul.

— ANONYMOUS

I USE A MIRROR TO SEE MYSELF, but the mirror reflects only the image I can see with all its imperfections. I'm sure that somewhere God is laughing at me. She laughs because she sees more than I do. She can see through me. As I turn away from the mirror, for the first time I see my self, my essence, and my beauty reflected in God's eyes.

Soulution of the Day

Reflect on the fact that you are much more than the physical being you see in the mirror. Stop judging and become a perfectly imperfect human being.

PETHERAPY

Were it only to learn benevolence to humankind, we should be merciful to other creatures.

— PLUTARCH

I TAKE OUR DOG, Furphy, everywhere I go. He is a little Lhasa apso and gets all the hellos and greetings when we are out.

In my therapy groups, he always knows when the sessions are over and lets me know it's time to take him for a walk. I point this out to the group members, hoping they will follow his example and learn to speak up when they have needs.

In one group, a man was sharing a tragic story about his cancer, when the room was filled with the sound of someone snoring. The speaker was very upset that someone would be so uncaring as to fall asleep while he was speaking about his anguish. When the listeners pointed to Furphy, the snoring culprit, the speaker and everyone in the room burst into laughter.

Furphy is an excellent therapist and knows when a good laugh is needed or when a little attention is necessary. God grant that some day we will be as kind to animals as they are to us.

Soulution of the Day

Adopt a pet or two and experience petherapy every day.

MEDITATION

*Meditate deeply... reach the depth
of the source. Branching streams cannot
compare to this source! Sitting alone
in a great silence, even though the
heavens turn and the earth is upset,
you will not even wink.*

— NYOGEN SENZAKI

LET CONSCIOUSNESS SPEAK to you of the wisdom within through meditation. Try meditating on these themes, which can help direct you:

- *See yourself as an acorn or seed of your choice growing and spreading your seeds.*

- *Imagine connecting your heart and head so their wisdom can be shared.*

- *See yourself as a ripple in a stream or a source of light, and notice how limitless your actions are.*

- *Think of your life as a river and see where this bloodstream began and where it's going.*

- *Go on a guided visualization; walk along the path of your life and meet guides who will help direct you.*

- *Go within your body and let it speak to you of its needs. Listen to your mind, body, heart, and spirit.*

There are no limits to the guidance that can come from the consciousness within you and its connection, through meditation, to the greater consciousness of creation.

Soulution of the Day

*Take the time to listen to the voice of creation
and connect with the universal consciousness.*

PLAY

*It's only work if there's someplace
else you'd rather be.*
— GEORGE HALLAS

WHAT DID YOU ENJOY DOING AS A CHILD? Find a way to bring that enjoyment back into your life. It is important to spend time playing each day. What you consider play may seem like work to others, but that is not the issue. How you define what you are doing is what matters.

Think of earning a living doing what you consider relaxing and playful. When you are doing what you love, you are contributing not only to the world but also to your own health.

I might have been an artist instead of a surgeon if I had known as a child that people bought paintings. I can't imagine a more joyful life than being paid for doing what you love to do; then you are never really working. I find that in many ways writing fits in this category. I learn while I write, and if my writing also helps others to cope with life, then we are all being given a gift. It isn't work, but love made visible.

One word about guilt: too often we are brought up to feel guilty playing and relaxing. I say to you, that's ridiculous! You and I know that on our deathbeds we are not going to be sorry for the time we spent playing and relaxing. But we will regret the time we didn't spend enjoying life with our loved ones.

Soulution of the Day

*Start noticing what "play" is for you.
Then allow yourself not to feel guilty doing what you enjoy.*

CREATING MIRACLES

Miracles happen to those who believe in them.

— **BERNARD BERENSON**

A TRUE MIRACLE is usually defined as an event that defies the laws of nature as we know them. On the other hand, quantum physicists reveal that desire and intention can alter the physical world. Thus reaching for the unreachable star makes sense, and creating miracles becomes possible, if one is willing to do the work.

I think we do not know our own potentials. We are all capable of creating miracles because of the nature of life, consciousness, and energy. When we reach for new heights, we can make a difference and create something of joy and wonder for ourselves and for those around us.

The miracles I hope for are not the ones that change the physical nature of life but the ones that change our experience of life. When we are ready to make a difference and create peace, love, and happiness for all living things, that will indeed be a miracle.

Soulution of the Day

What unreachable star are you shooting for?

PRESCRIPTION #21

SPIRITUALITY

Well and good if all things change,
Lord God, provided we are rooted in you.

— SAINT JOHN OF THE CROSS

WE NEED TO BRING SPIRITUALITY to earth and make it a part of our lives. In a sense, our life is our religion. As Mother Teresa said, "The essential thing is not what we say, but what God says to us and through us. All our words will be useless unless they come from within."

What matters is not spectacular actions, but the love you put into each action. If your actions are full of love for God, then you will do everything well. There are no separate faiths when you act out of love. There is only one religion, the essence of spirituality, which is love.

Your vocation becomes your way to bring God's love to the world. You are God with skin on. You are the wires through which the current flows. If the battery is not connected to the motor the car will not start. It is the same for us; if we are not connected to our Source, we cannot make our true journey.

Soulution of the Day

Start your life.
Connect with the Source and begin the journey of love.

WHAT'S IMPORTANT, WHAT'S NOT

By the time we hit fifty, we have learned our hardest lessons. We have found out that only a few things are really important. We have learned to take life seriously, but never ourselves.

— MARIE DRESSLER

LIFE OFTEN BECOMES EASIER the older you get because you begin to see what is important and what isn't. For instance, it becomes easier to watch and enjoy your children growing up rather than directing all their actions. If they are headed for a crash into a wall you learn to warn them, then step aside rather than get run over. You learn that worrying doesn't solve any problems.

Our oldest son asked me one day, "How come my brothers and sisters don't have to do all the things I had to do?" I answered, "It's because I've learned that some of the things I asked you to do aren't important." I have come to see that what is important to me is peace of mind.

Life offers many opportunities to differentiate between what is really important and what is simply an attempt to control circumstances that are beyond your control.

Soulution of the Day

What are some of the things you used to think were important?

What is important to you now?

If I asked you, "What do you want me to pray for in your life?" what would your answer be?

HAVE NO REGRETS

Regret for the things we did can be tempered by time; it is regret for the things we did not do that is inconsolable.

— SYDNEY J. HARRIS

YOU DON'T WANT TO LIVE IN SUCH A WAY that when your life is over you are left thinking more about what you *didn't* do than what you *did* do. Think about how you would feel on your deathbed if you were wishing you had done that one special thing or taken that chance that you let pass by.

From that perspective, examine your life today. Think about some risks you have been unwilling to take — perhaps changing careers, following a dream, opening your heart to another person, or being all you can be. You can do nothing to change the decisions you made in your past, but the future holds many opportunities.

I remember a college football player diagnosed with cancer who said to me, "Before I got cancer there were games where I could have given more of myself." He regretted that he had held back. From his battle with cancer, he learned to not leave anything in the locker room but to bring it all with him out on the field. We all need to "bring it all out on the field" of our lives. It is the only way not to have regrets. Let there be no "if only's" or "I wish I had's" in your life.

Soulution of the Day

Watch the movie Harold and Maude, *in which Ruth Gordon plays an eighty-year-old woman who says to a troubled young man, "Give me an L, give me an I, Give me a V, Give me an E. LIVE!"*

THE CAT'S MEOW

*There are two means of refuge
from the miseries of life: music and cats.*

— ALBERT SCHWEITZER

WHEN I HEAR THE SONG from the Broadway show *Cats* — "If you touch me, you'll understand what happiness is"— I totally agree with the sentiment. Being touched physically and emotionally is an important part of leading a healthy and happy life.

Animals and children know how to get love and attention. They cry out to be touched and petted. If they don't like your response they make noise, and if that doesn't work, they do something else. Sometimes when I'm at my computer our cats and dog will walk up and howl or nudge me until they get their backs rubbed. Even our house rabbit, Smudge, will grunt threateningly when I don't respond to her.

A hungry child that wants to be fed or a baby wishing to be held has no problem letting you know its feelings. How many adults do you know who are willing and brave enough to cry out to be touched? We need to learn how to ask for what we really need, just like children and animals do.

Soulution of the Day

*Every infant of every species knows how to call out and ask for love.
Learn from them; then you too will know true happiness.*

SLAY YOUR DRAGON

Fear makes men believe the worst.

— QUINTUS RUFUS,
ALEXANDER THE GREAT

I WOULD LIKE TO SHARE one of my favorite stories: "A young man enters a dark cave and discovers a treasure. When he walks forward to pick it up, he sees it is guarded by a dragon. He leaves the cave in fear for his life and then spends every day thereafter wishing he'd had the courage to pick up the treasure.

As an old man, he goes back to the cave to see the treasure once more before he dies. As he moves forward to look at it more closely, he sees that what he thought was a dragon is actually only a small lizard. He picks up the treasure and takes it home to his family."

I invited a ninety-year-old patient of mine to become a member of a support group I run for people with life-threatening illnesses. She asked me why I wanted her to join. I told her it was because of all the losses and illnesses she had experienced and overcome.

One day, when group members were expressing their deep fears, I turned to her and asked, "What are you afraid of?" After a long pause she said, "Oh, I know. Driving on the parkway at night." Her words were followed by a burst of laughter from the group as she helped them turn their dragons into lizards.

Soulution of the Day

*What dragons exist in your life because of perceived
limitations and fear? Take a chance. Reach out. You can't fail,
so don't wait until you're ninety to find your treasure.*

TURNING POINT

What if you gave someone a gift, and they neglected to thank you for it — would you be likely to give them another? Life is the same way. In order to attract more of the blessings that life has to offer, you must truly appreciate what you already have.

— RALPH MARSTON, *THE DAILY MOTIVATOR*

A GENTLEMAN I WAS TALKING TO on the phone related that his doctor and the EMR team had told him his heart stopped beating and he had died at least five times during surgery. He concluded our conversation by saying, "I used to have troubles, but now I have only blessings." His outlook clearly had been turned around by this experience.

I meditate each day, and one portion of the meditation consists of my thinking about what I am grateful for. Most of us never stop to consider our blessings; rather, we spend the day only thinking about our problems. But since you have to be *alive* to have problems, be grateful for the opportunity to have them. Some people use their problems to get attention and are afraid to give them up and be blessed. I prefer to appreciate life and accept my problems as a part of my life.

When my body gets to the point where I can no longer function or feel gratitude, then I'll leave it and become grateful again. But until then, I will appreciate what I have and not whine about what I don't have. I will feel blessed by life and the opportunity to help others see that they are blessed too. Blessings come in many shapes and sizes. Be prepared, as my gentleman caller was.

Soulution of the Day

*What gifts have I failed to see before me?
Don't wait for a disaster to awaken you to the things
you can be grateful for today.*

THE ELEVATOR

Friendship is a horizon — which expands
whenever we approach it.

— E. R. HAZLI

THE ELEVATOR DOOR OPENED, and I got on the elevator with three doctors. How did I know they were doctors? They didn't speak, smile, or acknowledge me. When we reached the lobby we parted as strangers.

To tell you the truth, I'd rather get on an elevator with three dogs. We'd bark, sniff, growl, and rub against each other... and maybe leave a few scents behind for the maintenance crew to deal with! Four friends would depart in the lobby promising to sniff each other out again.

Soulution of the Day

Today "sniff out" someone from your past.
Make a point to be open to others: don't shut them out.

HOPE

"Hope" is the thing with feathers —
That perches in the soul —
And sings the tune without the words —
And never stops — at all —

— EMILY DICKINSON

HOPE RESTORES US. What each of us hopes for will differ and change with time. I believe we need hope to go on living. Hope inspires us to reach for the future. It gives us something to look forward to and strive for on our path.

If we had no hope — for a cure, for winning the lottery, for falling in love, for the end of war, for being free of abuse, or for having food, warmth, clothing, and shelter — we would have no reason to go on. What you hope for doesn't matter, but rather the essence of hope itself.

I see people who die a few minutes after a doctor tells them there is no hope of a cure. They give up and go. Others get angry and find joy in proving the doctor wrong. Something within them is challenged and hopeful. Hope is the divine motivator.

Soulution of the Day

Allow the bird of hope to perch on a branch
of the tree of life and never stop singing.

REPEAT THE QUESTION

*Ask and it will be given to you; seek and you
will find; knock and the door will be opened
to you. For everyone who asks receives, he
who seeks finds; and to him who knocks, the
door will be opened.*

— MATTHEW 7:7–8

AUDIO RECORDINGS are often made of my lectures. At one conference audience members were given the opportunity to ask questions without speaking into a microphone. So that everyone could hear, the organizers held up a sign to remind me to "please repeat the question."

I asked for one of their signs to add to my collection, and I use them to reinforce points I make at other presentations. We all know the biblical saying, "Ask and you shall receive." Well, if you ever ask God for anything and don't get an answer right away, maybe you need to "please repeat the question." God has a busy schedule too!

I find when I repeat my question or request, it changes with time as I become more aware of what I truly need. So rethink it, clarify what you really are asking for, and you will receive what you need, in God's time.

Soulution of the Day

*Step up to the microphone and repeat your question so it gets heard
and recorded on God's answering machine. I guarantee you'll get an answer.
How God answers and who God uses to answer may surprise you.*

BUTTERFLY WINGS

*What the caterpillar calls the end of the
world, the Master calls a butterfly.*

— RICHARD BACH

WHEN CONFRONTED by a seemingly insurmountable challenge, my thoughts often turn to the caterpillar and the butterfly. The caterpillar faces a tremendous struggle to emerge from the cocoon, but it must make this effort in order to survive. It is the same with life. If we avoid the struggles, we may be doing ourselves more harm than good. We may never give birth to our true self.

Sometimes it is the struggle and the inherent growth in the process that propel us to where we need to be. Asking for help can be appropriate at times, but some things we must do for ourselves. If the butterfly is helped out of the cocoon it will not acquire enough strength to fly. Perhaps we too need the struggle in order to spread our wings and be transformed.

Soulution of the Day

*What strengths lie in the caterpillar of your existence?
What butterfly is waiting to be born?*

UNDERSTAND WHY

There are simply no answers to some of the great pressing questions. You continue to live them out, making your life a worthy expression of leaning into the light.

— ANONYMOUS

MANY YEARS AGO my great-grandfather told me of the persecution he experienced in Russia, which led him to come to this country. He said the Cossacks pursued him at night when he was out teaching and tried to slash him with their sabers. One night he was on the hill above his village with his rabbi, the Ba'al Shem Tov. As they looked below, they could see the Cossacks riding down and killing their fellow Jews. My great-grandfather heard the rabbi say, "I wish I were God." He asked, "Do you want to be God so you can change the bad into the good?"

"No, I wouldn't change anything. I want to be God so I can understand why," was the rabbi's reply.

As a physician I have also asked why. I have tried to understand why our Creator made the world the way it is, full of plagues, hatred, and troubles. Why do innocent children suffer? One day while I was meditating, an answer came to me. It turned out to be a simple one: "If I'd made a perfect world it would have been a magic trick and not creation. Creation is work." So we are here to work at creating a world where life takes on meaning because we are showing love and compassion as an act of free will.

Soulution of the Day

When questioning "why," seek the answer through the creation of meaningful works.

FORM AND ESSENCE

The more you depend on forces outside your-self, the more you are dominated by them.

— HAROLD SHERMAN

WHEN I WORK WITH PEOPLE in assisted-living facilities, I ask them to draw a picture of themselves today and twenty-five years ago. I almost always get a picture of a fat, unhappy person now and a slim, smiling one of earlier days.

The truth is that everyone, regardless of their age, tends to draw the same two pictures. I can recall looking at old home movies of our family and being amazed that I didn't look as bad as I remembered. Everyone else looked good too. I rarely find an individual who appreciates herself as she is now and as she was then.

Most of us get caught up in our form and appearance and spend a great deal of time and money to make ourselves look younger and more attractive. We are critical of the form that appears in the mirror, but within that human form lies something more, our essence. It is only when we see the beauty within that we come to know our true selves. When we realize that our essence is divine, we will see beauty wherever we look.

Although both are components of the same physical entity, form and essence are two very different things. Our form is a gift that allows us to manifest our essence. We need our body and all its problems to carry out the work of the divine. When our focus is constantly aimed at our outer world, it prevents us from spending our time cultivating that which nurtures our essence.

Soulution of the Day

Honor your total self. Life becomes meaningful and your purpose more clear when you come from a place of wholeness. Notice how much time you spend doing things that support your essence.

GUIDANCE AND FRIENDSHIP

Friendship is the golden thread
that ties all hearts together.

— ANONYMOUS

ONE DAY MARILYN, one of our support group members, sent me an email with the subject line *guidance*. In her email, she told me that the word *dance* being a part of the word *guidance* made her think about how dancing is like doing God's will. Two people dancing are not struggling with each other; one leads and the other willingly follows. When the two become a team their movements flow in harmony with each other.

When she looked back at the word she saw the *G* as representing God and then *U* and *I*. So guidance is about God, you, and I dancing together. When you are willing to trust and believe, guidance comes. I believe the rhythm we should all be dancing to comes from our Creator. It allows us to move as a team while creating our unique dance of life.

The thoughts she related in her email made me think about the word *friendship* as well. We are all sailing through the waters of life, which are sometimes turbulent and stormy and sometimes calm with the breeze at our backs. But no matter what the sailing conditions are, doing it with friends makes it easier.

So when you set sail, remember to bring some friends along. When things get rough you'll have the supporting crew who will help you through the storms, and when the wind fills your sails you'll have someone to share the joyful journey with.

Soulution of the Day

Sail through life knowing your guidance comes from the eternal compass, which knows the direction you must sail to return to your home port.

PRESCRIPTION #34

RELEASE THE PAST

We are taught you must blame your father, your sisters, your brothers, the school, the teachers — but never blame yourself. It's never your fault. But it's always your fault, because if you wanted to change, you're the one who has got to change.

— KATHARINE HEPBURN

MANY OF US USE OUR PAINFUL PASTS as a good excuse for accomplishing nothing. The pain can act as a dam that blocks the flow of your life or a painful burn that scars your existence.

You can use the pain and let it become the energy and passion that move you. The choice of how you use it is yours. Release the dam and use the energy of the released waters to propel you. Use the heat and light created by the flame to warm you and illuminate your way. Have the courage to break down the barriers and move forward.

It is easier to blame the past than to create your future. Where do you want to live: in the past or in the now, creating a better future?

Soulution of the Day

Hate and fear destroy life and keep us holding on to pain. Instead use the pain in your life to create something meaningful.

A BEST FRIEND

*Everyone is a bore to someone.
That is unimportant. The thing to avoid
is being a bore to oneself.*

— GERALD BRENAN

WHO IS THE MOST IMPORTANT PERSON in your life? Reflect on that question for a moment. The answer is *you*. No one can replace you. You need to be for yourself what we all need: a best friend, someone who can put up with your craziness and inadequacies but still accept you and be there for you.

Stop tearing yourself to pieces when others don't like something you've done. Even if what you did was wrong, dangerous, or stupid, it is the act, not *you*, that is the problem.

So do not let others destroy the relationship you have with the most important person in your life—you! Accept your uniqueness and free others to be themselves too.

Soulution of the Day

In what ways can you be a best friend to yourself today?

SERVICE

What is a deeply satisfying human life,
and how do we design one?

— LENEDRA J. CARROLL,
THE ARCHITECTURE OF ALL ABUNDANCE

WE ALL DESIRE A SATISFYING LIFE. How do we accomplish having one? There are many ways to seek satisfaction. We may try to get others to do things for us and yet that alone does not bring fulfillment. Another way we search is by trying to fill our lives with material possessions. But accumulating belongings is not what makes life satisfying. It may make the neighbors jealous, but it won't make your life meaningful or joyful.

Look at the wise words of the sages, who tell us to serve others, and you will find the eternal message about how to have a satisfying life. It is not about getting acknowledgment or thanks, but the inherent joy that comes from doing for others. Find your way of serving the world and giving it your love, and watch what it does for your life.

Soulution of the Day

Serve those in need, and receive the gift of life.

THE COVER-UP

*It's a mistake to think we listen only with our
ears. It's much more important to listen with
the mind, the eyes, the body, and the heart.
Unless you truly want to understand the
other person, you'll never be able to listen.*

— MARK HERNDON

PEOPLE ARE TRAINED TO COVER UP the truth about what they are
really feeling. We've all heard the messages: "Be strong, don't show
your feelings, don't let people see you like that," and so on. But
when people you know deny their troubles, you can tell if they are
speaking the truth by the way they express themselves. When we
really listen to each other, we are able to interpret the cover-ups and
see the truth underneath.

We need to look inside the lives of those we communicate with
and acknowledge what they are experiencing and feeling. So use
your insight, and when you sense a problem, speak up and offer to
help. Whether they accept your help or not is their choice.
However, your caring and willingness to be available will increase
the chances they will share their problems and start to heal.

Soulution of the Day

*The next time you ask someone how she is doing, close your eyes when she
answers and see through her shield of words with your insight.*

PRACTICE
OR TREAT

*Love and compassion are necessities,
not luxuries. Without them,
humanity cannot survive.*

— THE DALAI LAMA

ONE DAY I WAS THINKING about the difference between treating a disease and practicing medicine. When you treat a disease, you are not concerned with the person involved, but simply the diagnosis. You prescribe for the condition but ignore the person's experience.

This principle is the same for people of every profession — lawyer, roofer, plumber, or doctor. You can ignore the human aspect of your client/patient, make your diagnosis, and prescribe the appropriate treatment, without regard to what the person is feeling, experiencing, or the effect it is having on their bodies, minds, spirits, and financial well-being.

So you have a choice: to practice as an artist and help to heal lives or to treat as a technician and only deal with problems. Regardless of your profession, when you treat people with thoughtful consideration, the outcome will prove to be more lasting and beneficial.

Soulution of the Day

*When doing your job, practice the "art" of your profession
and care for the whole person.*

UNDER PRESSURE

*A diamond is just a piece of charcoal
that handled stress exceptionally well.*

— ANONYMOUS

MANY PEOPLE PAY CLOSE ATTENTION to all the TV commercials telling them how to avoid pain. But pain is the great unwanted therapist. It presses us to do something different.

A woman with a severe migraine headache of five days' duration was about to be admitted to the hospital. She described her pain as pressure and a weight on her head. I helped her deal with the pressures in her life, which were related to her marriage. In a few minutes the headache was gone, and she was on her way home, hopefully to change things and use the gift she had just received.

It is moments of passion and clarity like she experienced that create the desire, intention, and determination to make something happen. Don't fear or avoid your pain, for it might be the catalyst you need to help you release the dam and move you into healing.

Soulution of the Day

*Under pressure charcoal becomes a diamond.
Use your pain and the gifts it brings to change things
and create a gem out of your life.*

DOLPHINS AS HEALERS

To the dolphin alone, Nature has given that which the best philosophers seek: friendship for no advantage.

— **PLUTARCH,** *PEOPLE AND DOLPHINS*

WE ALL HAVE HEARD STORIES about the wisdom of dolphins, from how they have saved drowning people to their response toward the disabled who enter the aquarium water. Dolphins can detect differences in our energy and respond to that energy much more easily than we can. Science reveals a field of universal consciousness that can be measured by random energy generators. As humans, we have difficulty tuning into that energy because we think too much.

Several years ago a young woman with cancer I knew went to Florida to die. Her friends there worked with dolphins and disabled children, and they had her join the dolphins in the water. The dolphins treated her so gently it was obvious they knew of her affliction.

These same dolphins would swim over to a hemiplegic child and exercise its paralyzed limbs. How do they know about our afflictions and where they reside? Is it because our parts contain an energy that the dolphins can sense and communicate with? I believe so. I also believe we are all capable of sensing this energy. I often do when working with patients or healthcare professionals. I can sense who has a healing nature and will be therapeutic to the people they encounter and care for.

That young woman who swam with the dolphins called me one night to say she was having trouble dying. I answered that it would be easy when she was ready. I told her I had never had a call from a dolphin with that problem. She died peacefully that evening.

Soulution of the Day

Use all your senses and be open to the energy that surrounds you.

SAYING GOOD-BYE

The best part of a good man stays forever.
For love is immortal and makes
all things immortal.

— **WILLIAM SAROYAN**

MANY YEARS AGO, a patient of mine went to the Hawaiian island of Kauai to die. Her mother lived there, and my patient wanted to heal her relationship with her mother before she died.

Several years later I was invited to speak and present a workshop on the island. One day my wife and I entered a store and noticed a tiger swallowtail butterfly trapped in a large chandelier. My wife felt the need to rescue it, and so she climbed up on the counter and held out her hand to the butterfly, which flew onto her palm. Then she climbed down. We went outside to release it, but the butterfly wouldn't leave. My wife tried brushing it off of one shoulder, but it just flew to the other. So we stopped trying to brush it off and let it accompany us.

That night I said, "Bobbie, you need to let the butterfly go. We'll crush it if we take it to bed with us." She went out on the porch, returned, and said, "I brushed it off my shoulder." I said, "Honey, it's sitting on your other shoulder." We finally arranged a plate of sweet water on a kitchen counter, and the butterfly settled on its rim for the evening.

The next day, the butterfly hopped on and went to the workshop with us. I put it in a paper bag and planned to use it as part of my talk about life as a series of beginnings, not endings. After discussing the symbolism of the caterpillar and butterfly, I opened the bag and let our butterfly out to demonstrate. The butterfly spent the day overhead, and then left after the workshop.

Why did it spend so much time with us? My answer was that it represented the spirit and consciousness of my patient and was her way of thanking me and saying good-bye.

Soulution of the Day

Have you ever noticed what appeared to be signs or messages
from loved ones who passed away?

ARGUE OR LOVE

In arguments similes are like songs in love:
they describe much but prove nothing.

— **MATTHEW PRIOR**

SHALL WE ARGUE OR MAKE LOVE? Some believe there are benefits to both. If we argue I can show you how smart and right I am. I can yell and sulk, turn away, try to sleep, and act as if I've won. If we love, there are no words equal to the feeling. We will both sleep in peace because there are no losers, only winners who have chosen to give their victories away.

Soulution of the Day

Being right sometimes comes at a high price; the cost is your happiness.
Love is free and brings discount offers with it.

HOW DOES YOUR GARDEN GROW?

*And the time came when the risk to
remain tight in a bud was more painful
than the risk it took to blossom.*

— ANAÏS NIN

EACH CELL WITHIN US is like a wise seed capable of growth and blossoming. In nature seeds show their wisdom. Even when they are paved over, they know which direction is up. They intuitively grow up toward the light and life. They push their way through obstructions, deal with adverse weather, and cope with pests and poison in order to complete their mission here on earth.

Plants know that sometimes they must give up a part, be it by pruning or natural loss, to manifest their true beauty. They are not critical of their growth, nor do they compare themselves to others. While seeds don't have to think and worry about all the things we do, we must understand that like them sometimes we too have to fight our way through darkness to survive.

We have the wisdom to nourish our potential and reach for the light. We are capable of growth and have the ability to get through life's adversities. Even the "compost" in our lives could be better used if we would let it stimulate our growth rather than be buried beneath it. If we pay attention to our inner wisdom and nourish the seed within, there is no telling what we can blossom into during the seasons of our life.

Soulution of the Day

*Don't forget that seeds and plants also have quiet times in which they
restore and nourish themselves. How often do you take the time to
nourish, restore, and revel in your growth and to remember that
sometimes loss may lead to life-enhancing changes?*

A TO-DO LIST FOR GOOD HEALTH

If we don't change, we don't grow. If we don't grow, we aren't really living.

— GAIL SHEEHY

"IT'S KILLING ME." Yes, there are things that may kill us that we have no direct control over, but most of the time that expression relates to the things in our lives that we can act on and change: jobs, behaviors, attitudes, and more.

My suggestion is to make a list of what is "killing you" and decide what you want to do about it *now*. If you have trouble thinking about what should be on the list, ask your body to give you a few hints. Put the list on the refrigerator and start working on eliminating everything from your list. When that is done, replace it with a new list of what you need to shop for to enhance your life.

Soulution of the Day

Check your list daily. Reevaluate situations that seem impossible. Then take action to make the needed changes to save your life.

VALENTINE'S DAY

We are all born for love.
It is the principle of existence,
and its only end.

— BENJAMIN DISRAELI

WILL YOU BE MY VALENTINE? It is a gift of a lifetime to be acknowledged as worth loving by someone you know. That someone accepts you, your faults and imperfections, and transcends them all with a commitment to love you.

Why do we love? I believe the desire to love is wired into us from the time of our birth and that to love is not a choice. Whom we love does become a choice as we go from the openness and acceptance of childhood to the close-mindedness and restrictions of adulthood. It is fitting that we have a day when we must stop and think about who we love and acknowledge them. Love is necessary to our survival.

Soulution of the Day

Valentine's Day can be lived every day.

ONE FAMILY

*You must look into people,
as well as at them.*

— **G. K. Chesterton**

THE OTHER DAY I was on a hotel elevator when a couple walked in. We rode together for a few floors, and then I heard the husband say, "I think you need to change."

She said, "I think my clothes are all right."

I said, "Maybe he's not talking about your clothes." They stared at me in disbelief until they realized I was acting the part of a child, and then they laughed and we became family.

Soulution of the Day

*Wherever you are, wherever you go,
you will meet your sisters and brothers.*

CAGES

*You are today where your thoughts have
brought you; you will be tomorrow where
your thoughts take you.*

— JAMES ALLEN

ANIMALS ONLY LIVE IN CAGES when they are forced to. Watch caged animals. Their eyes lose any sign of light and life, while their bodies waste away. They are prisoners.

I believe as people we create our own cages. Then, once inside, we become the prisoners and think we are powerless to escape. In truth, we manufactured the cage and are the only ones who can break free.

It may be a prison we created in our mind, in perceived circumstances, or repressed emotions. To release ourselves, we must break in and unlock the confines of our mind and heart. If we are willing to feel our pain and look into our life, the bars will fall away, and we will be free.

Soulution of the Day

*Escape from the cage you have built around yourself.
Look inward for the answer and make the necessary changes
in your life to find your freedom.*

SEEKING GLORY

*How many cares one loses when one decides
not to be something but to be someone.*

— Coco Chanel

IF YOU CREATE A WORK OF ART or develop a successful business venture so that people will be impressed and admire what you have done, you are really only seeking personal gain. If you think of fulfillment as coming from impressing others, making money, seeing your name in the papers, or showing your parents that you are not a failure, you will be disappointed because it will not bring you happiness.

Happiness is an "inside job." Only by searching within can you truly find what will make you happy. So ask yourself these questions: Am I serving money, or am I serving God? Am I working at something to please my parents, or myself? Is what I'm doing serving humanity as well as myself? Ultimately you must ask yourself, "Who is my Lord? And who am I serving?"

Soulution of the Day

*Self-admiration and glory-seeking serve as signs
that you are not truly enlightened.*

SUDDENLY BECOME OLD

But maybe I ought to practice a little now?
So people who know me
are not too shocked and surprised
When suddenly I am old,
and start to wear purple.

— JENNY JOSEPH

MANY HAVE WRITTEN POEMS and stories about the freedom they give themselves when they grow old. You can be eccentric and get away with it because old age is an excuse and you no longer care about what people think.

But why wait to grow old to have the opportunity to live? Growing old can't be avoided unless you die at a young age, which is not a satisfactory alternative, as far as I am concerned. Why not enjoy life more now and prepare people for your even more bizarre actions when you do grow old? Why wait to shock them; start now!

I remember a woman in a support group complaining about the demands her family made on her. I told her to take care of herself and say no to them. She said, "You can't say no until you are eighty."

So I said, "Every Thursday act like you're eighty." She liked the idea and gave it a try.

Soulution of the Day

Start acting like you have suddenly become old at least one day a week.

SURVIVAL BEHAVIOR

With love anything is possible.

— **ANONYMOUS**

A FRIEND OF MINE learned she had a short time to live. To have some company for the last few months of her life, she adopted a stray cat. She took it to the vet to be sure it was healthy. Lo and behold, it had feline leukemia and had a year to live. Upon returning home my friend was devastated and depressed, but the cat wasn't. Thank God she learned from the cat because, as I write this, it is fourteen years since that day, and they both have survived.

Animals respond to love, live in the moment, express feelings, and in general know how to be survivors. I know of a cat in renal failure that was taken home to die and given special attention and love in preparation for his departure. Four years later he is still living.

I have gone through this with our own pets. When our children wouldn't let me have one of our pets euthanized, I saw firsthand what love can do. Our vet said, "I have never seen a dog this sick survive." Yet Oscar did for three good years. What can we learn from this? To never give up and never stop loving.

Soulution of the Day

Live in the moment and love with every breath.
Your life will have meaning, and you'll help lead the way for others.

TORCHBEARER

To you from failing hands we throw the torch; be yours to hold it high.

— JOHN MCCRAE

AT NIGHT WE ARE SEEING LIGHT that originated billions of years ago. Light has no limits. When we shine, we have no limits either.

So become a luminary and light the way. Do not be afraid to pick up the torch and light the darkness. There are no limits to the effects your enlightened behavior will have.

Yes, it takes a certain energy and passion to light the darkness, but we are all capable of it when we shed our fears. By shining your light you can help others to heal as individuals and as inhabitants of this planet. So light your torch and illuminate the path. And if you see someone holding a torch who is old and tired or is wounded and falters, pick it up and carry on. Your life will have meaning and you'll help lead the way for others.

Soulution of the Day

Pick up the torch and move forward.
Do not fear the heat or being burned.

COMPASS

People trip not on mountains;
they stumble on stones.

— **HINDUSTANI PROVERB**

WHAT KEEPS YOU HEADED IN THE RIGHT DIRECTION? What compass have you chosen to guide you through life? Are your decisions related only to your desires?

I was brought up to do what made me happy when decisions confronted me. This was not about selfishness or self-interest; rather, it was about serving the world and living my life in a way that felt right for me.

It is not an accident that the word *compassion* is 70 percent *compass*. When we let compassion be the guide, we will be serving ourselves as well as those who need to be served. Let compassion direct you. It will also direct others to you when you encounter a time of need.

When you let compassion guide you, you can close your eyes, walk in the dark, and be sure of being on the right road. That is the internal compass that we all need in life. If that doesn't work try *com*plaining all the time. It's only 40 percent compass, but it's your choice.

Soulution of the Day

Tune into your internal compass.
What direction is it pointing in?

WASH AWAY YOUR WORRIES

For whatever we lose (like a you or a me)
it's always ourselves we find in the sea

— E. E. CUMMINGS

WHEN YOU ARE FEELING TROUBLED, it always helps to go down to the water. Water is a source of life and quite often holds the answers you seek. You can build a bridge over troubled waters and move on with your life, or you can let the waters wash away your troubles.

I love the beach and feeling of nearness to creation that it brings me. Go down to the beach at low tide and write your worries in the sand. After you have written every one down, sit quietly and visualize all the things on the list until the tide starts to come in. When it does, it will erase your worries one by one. Let them go as each one is washed away by the sea. If one resurfaces later, or you can't get down to the ocean, just picture the waves washing away your troubles with the tide.

You can cleanse your mind, body, and life in this way. Just as the tide never stops coming and going, you have the ability to continue to cleanse and heal. Let the water wash all your cares away.

Soulution of the Day

Visit the beach in person or in your mind as often as you need
until the ebb and flow of the tide cleanses your spirit.

MOMENTS OF MEANING

*The least of things with a meaning
is worth more in life than the greatest
of things without it.*

— C. G. JUNG

THINK BACK TO A TIME that was meaningful for you. I didn't say pleasant or joyful, I said meaningful. More often the meaningful events are not pleasant ones, but painful or frightening. Other times they are sudden epiphanies that bring great insight. Initially the incident may seem insignificant, and the full impact of it will not come until later. The meaningful moments focus us on the significance of our lives and how we spend our time.

How have these events become your teachers and guides? What lessons have you learned that have led you to where you are and the person you have become? Many times we have no idea how the decisions and choices we make lead us to experiences that become life altering.

Today, ask yourself what motivates you, what gives your life meaning? Find the answer, and you will find yourself. Look back at meaningful events; think about what gave you joy as a child. When you combine these two things, you will be living the life intended for you.

Soulution of the Day

*Today take the time to explore what is meaningful for you.
Ponder past events and note the lessons that they brought you.*

PATIENCE

*It is our impatience
that spoils things.*

— MOLIÉRE

I ONCE HEARD A STORY about a woman's husband who had returned from the war with post-traumatic stress syndrome. She was unable to deal with him or get him to care for himself and was ready to leave him. But first she sought the help of a healer.

The healer told her she could make a potion to heal her husband, but it required the chest hair of a bear.

The woman spent months befriending a bear at its cave. She brought it food and was able to get closer and closer until one day she was close enough to pull the hair and run for safety. She then brought the hair to the healer.

The healer threw the hair into the fire. The woman screamed, "I risked my life for that hair. You were to make a potion to heal my husband."

The healer smiled and said, "Now go home and be as patient with your husband as you were with the bear." The ability to wait patiently for something is a valuable character trait. It allows the other person time to know themselves and to heal. The only exception is when the other person's behavior threatens your well-being.

Soulution of the Day

Think about the proverb "Patience is a virtue."

TEARS

*God washes the eyes by tears until
they can behold the invisible land
where tears shall come no more.*

— HENRY WARD BEECHER

WHY WERE WE MADE WITH THE ABILITY TO CRY? A laugh feels good, and we never question its value, but why tears? We are born with the ability to cry tears because of the cleansing nature of water. What softens a dry, hard sponge? What cleanses a wound and washes away the dirt? I could go on forever asking questions about what water can do. It is necessary for life, and so are tears.

Emotions held within destroy us, but those that are washed away with tears restore us. Think of a sponge lying dried up and hard on the kitchen counter. If you didn't shed tears, that would be you. But if you plunge the sponge into warm water, it softens, just as we do when we are willing to cry tears of pain, joy, love, and acceptance.

Soulution of the Day

*Cleanse yourself with a good cry and let others know
it is all right for them to do the same thing.*

SLED DOG

*The journey is your goal
and your work is your path.*

— LAO-TZU

A FRIEND WHO SENT ME AN EMAIL used the metaphor of a sled dog as a reflection of our own inner guidance. The lead dog knows its way and follows its intuition when making decisions about crossing ice or finding a new path.

We have that wisdom in us too. I think our heart is our sled dog and knows the way for us to go. The key is to follow that wisdom and not stop or be diverted along the way to another path, as you would if you didn't trust your lead sled dog.

What kind of dog would you want as your lead dog, and what would you name it? Now give that image to your heart and call it by its new name. When the two of you are journeying together through new territory and emotions, remember to let your heart-dog lead.

Soulution of the Day

Remember that dogs like treats and long walks.

PRESCRIPTION #58

GRACE

Amazing grace how sweet the sound...
Was blind, but now I see.

— JOHN NEWTON

GRACE: even the word feels good to say, and I love the song "Amazing Grace." Someone I knew made the statement that they did not like to sing, "That saved a wretch like me." He preferred to sing, "That saved a soul like me." But isn't grace all about seeing beyond our human faults and imperfections?

When I can accept that I am a wretch in certain ways (and my wife can certainly add to that list) and then receive the grace of God, it truly means something to me.

If I were a glorious soul free of blemishes, of course I would expect salvation to come my way. But when I am a wretch, lost and bound in knots, and grace is bestowed on me, that is truly special.

Soulution of the Day

By the grace of God help yourself and others to be free.

STRADIVARIUS

*Rather than becoming tangled up
in all of the disturbances which endlessly
and infinitely present themselves in the field
of our worldly life, please let's consider
the preciousness of this life.*

— SWAMI CHETANANANDA

IF YOU WERE GIVEN A ROLLS ROYCE, a Stradivarius, a precious jewel, or something else of great value, how would you take care of it? I think the answer is obvious. You would guard it and care for it to maintain its value.

You are given a life to care for — your own. How do you take care of it? I think the answer is that sometimes you do not care for it as well as you do your other treasures. Every life is a beautiful instrument and work of art. Learn to use it and play it with all your talent. But most of all, treat your life with the respect it deserves.

You may not have been treated like a treasured instrument, but it is never too late to polish your finish and tune your strings. When you are in tune with the preciousness of life, teach others what you have learned.

Soulution of the Day

*You are a Stradivarius.
Play from your heartstrings.*

LONELINESS

*The eternal quest of the individual
human being is to shatter
his [or her] loneliness.*

— NORMAN COUSINS

WHEN YOU KNOW YOURSELF, you will never be lonely because you will always have yourself to be with. When you achieve this state of self-awareness you will also realize that there is a greater awareness, the universal consciousness that is aware of you and with you at all times. One of the ways to connect with this consciousness is through prayer. It can connect you with all things.

You have to be willing to see beyond yourself for this to happen. If you blame others for your loneliness or the lack of attention you receive, things will not change. Then loneliness will prevail. But if you focus on getting to know yourself and your Creator, you will always have company.

Soulution of the Day

*Take some time to get to know yourself better.
Keep a journal, meditate, pray, and listen.*

TEST QUESTIONS

*The foolish man seeks happiness
in the distance, the wise grows it
under his feet.*

— JAMES OPPENHEIM

HERE ARE SOME TEST QUESTIONS to see how you're spending your time on earth.

What is one thing you love about being alive?

How would you finish this sentence:

Thank God I'm _____?

How long did it take you to answer each question? If you had to stop and think, you took too long. These answers should flow easily. If they don't, it is a sign you're not in touch with your heart and that it needs to be nourished.

Now answer this question:

When you look at a garden do you see the weeds or the flowers?

If you had trouble with the answer, perhaps it is because you need to take off the blinders others have put over your eyes. You do not have to see what they tell you is before you. You have a choice in how you perceive your world. The true answers to all of these questions can only come from your heart.

Soulution of the Day

*Write down the first two questions.
For the next week respond to them with at least one new answer each day.
They are good questions to ask yourself on a monthly basis.*

PHOTOGRAPHS

*When the disposition charms
the features are pleasing.*

— OVID

I KEEP PHOTOGRAPHS of our entire family all around the house. Every generation can be viewed, no matter what room I enter. I do this because I love the people in those photographs, and their faces remind me of how much I in turn am loved.

In the kitchen, next to the phone, are two photos. One is of my wife's beautiful smiling face and the other is of me as a child. My wife's photo makes me fall in love with her every time I sit at the desk to write or answer the phone. It washes away all the problems of the day and serves as my therapist.

The picture of me is a photograph used in an advertisement when I was young. When my grandmother learned I was to be a model, she took all my clothes and ironed them. She turned them all inside out so the iron wouldn't burn or mark them. Well, the crease in the pants was reversed and it spoiled all the pictures. But they sure remind me of how much my grandmother loved me, and it helps me put up with myself.

Soulution of the Day

*Remind yourself of who you love by surrounding yourself
with their photographs. And don't forget to include one of yourself.*

PRESCRIPTION #63
BE WOLFLIKE

We listened for a voice crying in the wilderness. And we heard the jubilation of wolves.

— DURWARD L. ALLEN

HOW CAN YOU LIVE A FULL AND VITAL LIFE? In her book *Women Who Run with the Wolves: Myths and Stories of the Wild Woman Archetype,* Clarissa Pinkola Estés shares the "Wolf Rules" for life: "Eat, rest, rove in between, render loyalty, love the children, cavil in the moonlight, tune your ears, attend to bones, make love and howl often."

Sounds good to me!

So reconnect to your basic instincts and when in doubt, bring out the wolf in you.

Soulution of the Day

Make love and howl often!

LET GOD

*The mind is its own place and in itself can
make heaven of hell or a hell of heaven.*

— JOHN MILTON

WHAT DOES IT TAKE for some finally to let go and let God? Perhaps the following scenario: you are close to death, have lost everything, don't know where to turn, and are ready for death, so you let go and let God. I think most of us have to be at that point to be ready to let go. Until then we are finding time to worry about the crazy meaningless things that occupy our lives.

When the moment comes that you truly let go, you will find an inner peace beyond anything you have ever experienced. At that point you will be healed.

Stop for one moment as you read this and just sense turning everything over to a higher authority, a higher form of consciousness or wisdom, or whatever you may call it. Sense what doing so immediately does for you. That gift is always available if you can bring yourself to let go.

Soulution of the Day

*You cannot control anything but your thoughts.
So why not let go of trying to control what isn't yours
to control to begin with.*

PRESCRIPTION #65

I FEEL

There is a silence into which the world cannot intrude. There is an ancient peace you carry in your heart and have not lost.

— A Course in Miracles

I

I feel

I feel alive

I feel my heart beating

I feel my life and body dance to its rhythm

I feel my heartbeat

I feel my heart

I feel my life

I feel alive

I feel

I

Soulution of the Day

Attune yourself to the rhythms of your heart and life. Listen to the beat of your own drummer.

GOD KNOWS

*God's wisdom is manifold because
God is inexhaustible in His wonder,
and in His mercy.*

— JOHN ADAM WOODS

ONE DAY I WAS OUT WALKING with a friend on his Florida farm. As we walked he began to question God's wisdom in creating things as they were. He pointed out how large pumpkins were growing on a thin vine while lemons and oranges were hanging from large trees. I didn't have an answer and just continued to walk and enjoy the scenery.

We came to an area where his field hands were picking the fruit from the trees. We stood, watched, and continued to talk. The men began to work on a tree we were standing beneath, and several pieces of fruit fell, one hitting my friend on the head!

I laughed and said, "Well, now you know that God doesn't make mistakes, and has a reason for everything."

He said, "What are you talking about?"

I answered, "Supposing that had been a pumpkin that landed on your head."

I think he got the message!

Soulution of the Day

*There is a reason for everything, whether we can figure it out or not.
Imagine if a pumpkin had fallen on Isaac Newton!*

INTRODUCTIONS

No man is an island, entire of itself;
every man is a piece of the continent.

— JOHN DONNE,
DEVOTIONS UPON EMERGENT OCCASIONS

THE OTHER DAY I introduced my right hand to the rest of my body. I thought they ought to know each other better. Perhaps you're thinking, "That's crazy! They already know each other. They are all part of the same thing, made of the same thing, come from the same thing. They don't need an introduction."

Well, when I get to Heaven and they ask me if I want to be introduced to God, I'll say, "That's crazy! We already know each other. We are part of the same thing, made of the same thing, come from the same thing. I don't need an introduction. Just tell Him his right hand is here."

Soulution of the Day

We are all part of God's world,
so in truth we don't need an introduction.

DEATH

The perfection of moral character
consists in this, in passing every day
as the last.

— MARCUS AURELIUS

OUR CULTURE TRIES VERY HARD TO DENY DEATH. We don't say people died; rather, we say they failed, kicked the bucket, went to a better place, passed on, expired, and so on. I once had a textbook with two pages devoted to how to say someone died without using the word *died*.

Plastic surgery, medications, and other things are ways to deny the aging process. But the truth is, you don't start living until you accept your mortality. As long as you think you have an unlimited time ahead, you don't worry about what you are doing. You act as if you'll have time for everything, but actually you may find you've missed out on the most important things.

There is an old Native American saying about carrying death on your shoulder to remind you to live in the moment. I think it is very wise.

Soulution of the Day

Live with the knowledge of your mortality.

SPRING

Every oak tree started out
as a couple of nuts
who stood their ground.

— HENRY DAVID THOREAU

SPRING HAS AN INTERNAL ENERGY that it stores within ready to leap forth, bloom, and blossom. In the spring the death rate goes down as people see the signs of rebirth and new life before them.

One year I watched a skunk cabbage break through a newly paved area and burst forth into the sunlight. I took my family to the site to introduce them to the cabbage so it could be an inspiration for them. I wanted them to face life's roadblocks with the wisdom, courage, and determination of the skunk cabbage seed.

Think for a moment. You are paved over and buried in the cold and dark. Is there hope? What are the survival statistics? Which way is up? What do you do when you hit the wall? Well, a seed doesn't worry about things the way we do. It starts moving toward the light and then meets the pavement. Does it quit? Does it give up and die? No!

When we live with determination, we will spring forth and find the light. Let us remember the message of spring and the seed of life contained in each of us.

Soulution of the Day

When confronted by obstacles, let the wisdom within guide you to the light.
Remember, like the song says, under the bitter snow
is a seed which in the spring will become a rose.

FAILURES

A life spent in making mistakes
is not only more honorable
but more useful than a life spent
doing nothing.

— GEORGE BERNARD SHAW

A YOUNG MAN once went to get advice from a famous businessman, a multimillionaire, who told the young man that he just hadn't failed enough times yet. This might seem like strange advice, but you need to keep failing until you succeed.

We always worry about what people will say about our failures. If Thomas Edison had worried about what people said he never would have invented the electric lightbulb. He failed so many times it is a wonder he believed he could actually create one. You need to believe in yourself and what you choose to do in order to succeed as he did.

Even if all you do is prove what won't work, you have accomplished something. When you stop being afraid of making mistakes and of failures, you become a productive human being and not simply a human "doing."

Soulution of the Day

Don't let your so-called mistakes and failures stop you
from moving forward. Go ahead, take a risk,
and remember that each failure brings you closer to success.

CONNECTIONS

*Give one another of your bread,
but eat not of the same loaf.*

— **KAHLIL GIBRAN**, *THE PROPHET*

OUR CONNECTIONS and relationships keep us alive and give our
lives meaning. The reason a woman with the same disease as a
man lives longer is that women tend to make more connections
in their lives. Married men live longer and are less likely to
develop lung cancer than single men smoking the same number of
cigarettes. Pet owners live longer too, and even those living in
nursing homes who feel responsible for caring for a plant live
longer than those who are given plants but no responsibility.

The key is to be connected but not attached. You must wean
yourself from attachments so that you can live your life with the
connections you desire, not attachments that restrict you.

Connections allow for communication and sharing, like when
you make a phone call and feel connected to someone. But when you
are attached to that person, you can never hang up. Attachments
will drain you; connections are gratifying and will give your life
meaning.

Soulution of the Day

*Reach out and connect with those around you,
but be conscious of when it is time to let go.*

NEGLECT

Self-love, my liege,
is not so vile a sin as self-neglect.

— **WILLIAM SHAKESPEARE**

TO NEGLECT ONE'S SELF is a sin and a purposeless act of destruction. No matter what others have done to you, you are worth loving. To abuse yourself while you care for other living things makes no sense.

You are a child of God, as we all are. Jesus, in the Gospel of Saint Thomas, said, "If you know who you are, you will become as I am." Invest in loving yourself. Begin to see yourself in a new way. It may be uncomfortable at first if you have never experienced love. But you are worth loving; I can assure you of that. It is not about ego inflation, it is about your true sense of worth.

Soulution of the Day

Notice the ways in which you neglect yourself.
Then make a list of small steps you can take to begin to nurture yourself.

TO DREAM

*Go confidently in the direction
of your dreams. Live the life
you have imagined.*

— HENRY DAVID THOREAU

IF WE DID NOT DREAM we would be living without hope. We must dream of what can be and not say why it is impossible. We must not deny ourselves the chance to dream and change the world in a positive way.

Dreaming lets us be insane creatively. The mind can create a script, and we can follow it. But dreams alone are not enough. If dreams are to come true one must act. Sitting around dreaming will not change the world.

Think of Martin Luther King Jr. dreaming of someday living in a world where we are all men and women are treated as equals or the Wright brothers believing they would fly. We all need to act to make our dreams come true.

Soulution of the Day

*Whether you daydream or you dream at night,
when you are finished, get up and do something to realize your dream.*

THE NEWS

No news is good news!

— **ANONYMOUS**

NEVER WATCH THE NEWS before you go to bed, after you wake up, or during the day, and you'll live a longer, healthier life. If you don't believe me, give up listening to, watching, and reading the news for one week and see how you feel. And think of all the free time you'll have to enjoy yourself! Don't worry: you'll hear about anything really important from someone in your life.

Why can't we have a good news station telling us about all the good deeds that people do? Occasionally if the kindness shown is really off the chart it does make the news, but only rarely. Think of what it does to our children to be exposed to the horrors of life every day. How will they act, and what will they believe when they get older?

Let me give you a bit of news. God loves you, and so do I. Now spread that news.

Soulution of the Day

*Try no news for one week. If by accident you hear or observe it,
do not discuss it. Take note on how you feel, sleep,
and what you accomplish that week.*

PRESCRIPTION #75

UPRIGHT

*Spiritual strength
depends on spiritual posture.*

— **RABBI LAIBL WOLF**

WHY IS MAN'S POSTURE UPRIGHT while most of the animal world's posture is horizontal? Why is our spine built to have us walk on two legs instead of four? Maybe it is a sign of what our lives should be like. Perhaps we should be reaching for a higher level of living and not just living by instinct, as other animals do.

Our spine also reminds us of the balance between those at the top and those at the bottom. This is not about evaluating the importance of an individual life but understanding that we are all important and that we all rely on each other. The head cannot go anywhere unless the feet carry it.

The key is to be aligned in an upright position and work to accomplish higher things with our lives.

Soulution of the Day

*Become upright in your life, relationships, and work.
If you need help, find a spiritual chiropractor.*

GIVING LOVE

*It's not how much we give
but how much love we put into giving.*

— MOTHER TERESA

AT ONE TIME I was caring for a teenage girl who had fallen into a fireplace and had been scarred by the burns. She yelled, "I hate you" at me every day when I dressed her wounds. It pained me to hurt her, and there was nothing I could do to make the scars go away. Several months later, on a scorching summer day, she came into the office in a long-sleeved turtleneck. I asked, "Why are you dressed like that on such a hot day?"

"Because I am ugly," she replied.

Then I asked, "What are you going to do this summer?"

"Nothing," she said.

"I know a nursing home that needs aides. Would you consider working there?"

She took the job not knowing that she would have to wear an outfit with short sleeves and a normal neckline. Weeks later when I saw her in the office I asked how things were going and if anyone had asked about her scars. She replied, "No one noticed."

I said, "When you are giving love, you are beautiful."

A few years later the young lady called me and said, "My dad died and I am getting married. I want you to be my chosen dad." I cried and answered, "Yes." At the wedding we danced to Kenny Rogers singing, "Through the years you never let me down. You turned my life around."

Soulution of the Day

*Today, instead of hiding behind your "scars"
find some way to give love and become beautiful.*

RHYTHM AND PACE

*Rhythm is the foundation and the
most essential element of any art form.
Its essence is pulsations, and therefore
movement, the basis of life itself.*

— PIA GILBERT AND AILEEN LOCKHART,
MUSIC FOR DANCE

WE EACH NEED to find a sense of rhythm to make our life flow.
The pace is also vital. The ticking of a clock at sixty beats a minute
quiets us, and so does music at that beat. Faster-paced pieces often
make us restless or hyperactive.

So find your rhythm and the intensity of the sound you are
comfortable with. If you are comfortable working a jackhammer,
fine. A cricket chirping might disturb someone else. Nothing is
right or wrong if you are living the rhythm of your life.

Connection and continuity are absent when someone or something else dictates the pace of your life's music. When you find the
rhythm that is right for you, your life will flow from one moment
to another.

Soulution of the Day

*Find your beat and conduct your life
as you would a musical composition.*

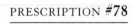

IRISH BLESSING

*There is no language like the Irish
for soothing and quieting.*

— JOHN MILLINGTON SYNGE

I THINK I WAS AN IRISH KNIGHT in a past life, but my name then was Brady, not Bernie. I have a love for many Irish things. The following Irish prayer and its words can guide you through life.

> *May the road rise to meet you*
> *May the wind be always at your back*
> *May the sun shine warmly on your face*
> *May the rain fall gently on your fields*
> *And may God hold you in the palm of His hand*
> *   until we meet again.*

Nothing is totally at our command; only our prayers can make a difference. I pray that you be blessed in this way, and I ask that you pray for all your loved ones and all the inhabitants of this blue planet.

Soulution of the Day

When life presents your loved ones with a drought,
be the water that sustains them and let your hand shade them from the heat.

PRESCRIPTION #79

FAVORITE FLOWER

*Little flower, but if I could understand,
what you are, root and all in all,
I should know what God and man is.*

— ALFRED, LORD TENNYSON

WE ARE ALL FLOWERS. What makes life so interesting is our variety. Think about your favorite flower and why it is your favorite. When you have finished listing its qualities, you will find you are talking about yourself.

I believe it is through nature that we come to see our beauty and finer qualities. Spending time in nature also helps us to find the answers to some of life's difficulties.

Once when I was wondering how to continue helping people without traveling, since I was tired of leaving home, I asked nature what to do. A flower showed me the answer. It told me, "I do not leave the place of my origin. I spread my seeds and let others help by carrying them to distant places."

So through this book, my words, an email, or a lecture, I am planting seeds of healing. Now I assign you to become like your favorite flower and spread your seeds of faith, hope, and love.

Soulution of the Day

*Think about the qualities of your favorite flower.
Then seed the earth with those things you admire.*

BEING RIGHT

*Indeed, this need of individuals
to be right is so great that they are
willing to sacrifice themselves,
their relationships, and even love for it.*

— REUEL HOWE

MANY PEOPLE CHOOSE to be right rather than happy. They will argue to the bitter end about the "rightness" of their thoughts and actions. They do not care about what they are doing to the people they are arguing with.

Why do they behave this way? Are they perfect? No, few of us could claim to be that. They are simply unwilling to view their fallibility and confess to the weaknesses that come along with being human.

When you are willing to give up being right, you will find peace and happiness. It is when you are ready to learn that you will be right.

Soulution of the Day

*If you wish to be happy and free,
give up having to be right all the time.*

ROOTS AND BRANCHES

A tree who may in summer wear,
a nest of robins in her hair.
A tree whose hungry mouth is pressed
against the earth's sweet flowing breast.

— JOYCE KILMER

A TREE IS A MAGNIFICENT LIVING THING. The other night I took the right wrong turn on the way to a support group meeting and ended up driving by the oldest tree in Connecticut, which was all lit up by spotlights. It is over two hundred years old, and its branches are truly amazing.

Think of a tree's life. It starts out with roots that grow into the ground and firmly hold the earth in their grasp. The roots nourish the tree so branches can grow and ascend into the heavens. The communication throughout the tree flows easily.

The roots and the branches do not waste time resenting each other because of their different exposures, functions, and purposes. Humans, on the other hand, sometimes fail to see how all their parts work together for the whole.

How are we, as people, able to have ground support as we reach for the stars and heavens above us? When we accept that we are part of a structure that must be unified if it is to survive, then like the tree our branches will truly reach to heaven.

Soulution of the Day

Let the sap within you circulate, nourish, and connect your life.
Unite body, mind, and spirit. Grow, branch out, and blossom.
Reach for the sky!

AFFIRMATIONS

*The artist does not see things
as they are, but as he is.*

— ALFRED TONNELLE

WE ARE WHAT WE BELIEVE OURSELVES TO BE. When we have grown up with negative messages emphasizing that we are incapable, uneducated, clumsy individuals who will fail at anything we attempt, then we work hard at living up to that image. After all, doing so frees us from having to accomplish anything and allows us to go about saying, "That's my nature" or "It's not my fault."

You can blame your life on your genes, parents, inadequate schooling, poverty, poor nutrition, or a million other things. Or you can get off your butt and affirm that you are a divine creature with enormous potential. Think of all the people in the world who have done just that. They overcame their difficult pasts and went on to follow their dreams. Some even risked their lives to fly into space, climb a mountain, or hike to the polar regions.

Find the artist within and affirm that you are capable of doing what you never thought you could accomplish. You have all the right stuff!

Soulution of the Day

*Look at the work of art that is reflected back when you see yourself
in the mirror; then affirm whatever it is you want to accomplish.
Use these affirmations to guide you to
a new way of seeing your life.*

FOCUS

The man who lives for self alone,
lives for the meanest mortal known.

— JOAQUIN MILLER

MY CAMERA HAS AN AUTOMATIC FOCUS. I point it at something, and it focuses on it. It doesn't argue with me, turn away, go out of focus, or refuse to see what is right before it.

People, on the other hand, often refuse to focus on what matters. We become so intent on our own needs and what we want that we can't see what is right in front of us. Life becomes way out of focus. What makes us, as humans, begin truly to focus? Sometimes it takes coming face-to-face with the reality that we will not live forever. Then we start to appreciate what is before us rather than what we want to see.

Cameras see all that exists through one lens. People need to expand their views and see things clearly without first running them through their various filters and colored lenses.

Soulution of the Day

Throw away your filters and stay focused on life and truth.

THE BARRIER BEACH

*To offer no resistance to life
is to be in a state of grace, ease, and lightness.*

— **ECKHART TOLLE**, *THE POWER OF NOW*

The barrier beach makes us feel safe, protected
But the sea accepts no barriers.
The shore gives, withdraws, shifts.
It achieves grace and beauty:
Gorgeous curves, secret islands,
Everything fits; everything is in its place.
Only the barrier beach stands straight and long against the sea.
It doesn't fit, it is hard and straight.
Life is relentless like the sea,
Its waves beating a constant path.
Let go, soften, shift, blend, be a part of life.
Feel the pulse, live it.
The barrier is a barrier to life.
Cancer is a barrier;
Hard when you hold it in your hand.
Growing it does not protect you, it hides your beauty.
Remove the barrier, let life be exposed.
Grow, love, weather the forces of nature.

Soulution of the Day

*Offer no resistance. Let life pound you with its waves until your barriers are
worn away. Flow with its tides and become one with the ocean.*

TEMPLES

Gone is the builder's temple
crumpled into the dust.

— HATTIE VOSE HALL

IF I ASKED YOU WHAT YOUR TEMPLE IS, what would you answer? Do you see your body and the bodies of your children and loved ones as temples?

I know a poem about two temples, one built by a builder and the other by a mother. It reminds me that if the temples we build are purely physical structures, buildings, or bodies, we must be prepared for their demise some day. The builder's temple will collapse, as will all the mechanical things in our lives, including our bodies.

But within the body the mother built is an immortal soul that will go on forever unburdened by time and that will continue to build on what the mother created. It may not be as obvious to the eye, but the loving care with which each stone was laid and her careful planning will produce a temple that will survive the death of the body.

Soulution of the Day

Put your effort into building an immortal structure.

RIVER OF LIFE

We are one with each other
as the waves are one with the ocean.

— ANONYMOUS

I ALWAYS THINK OF THE RIVER OF LIFE as our bloodstream, one that flows into the sea of eternity. Nothing really ends, it just changes form.

But if your life is a river, stop and think about where the source is. You were given a beginning and a life by the flow from others. Then which way did your river go? What has deepened it? Dammed it? Created turbulence? Calmed it? Warmed it? Lived within it? What has joined it, and what has it joined? Where is it going? What has it tumbled over?

This is your life. Are you finding your way or letting others direct the flow? Yes, we all must interact and change directions at times, but it is vital to maintain our own way. When you are depleted because of a drought in your life, remember you can be replenished by the waters from above. Go to a higher source.

Soulution of the Day

Your bloodstream is unique while still
a part of the great sea of life.

ACCENTUATE THE POSITIVE

Flatter me, and I may not believe you.
Criticize me, and I may not like you.
Ignore me, and I may not forgive you.
Encourage me, and I will not forget you.

— WILLIAM ARTHUR WARD

YOU MAY REMEMBER A LINE FROM AN OLD SONG that says to accentuate the positive and eliminate the negative. Have you made those words a part of your life? When you are talking to someone you love, do you criticize her behavior? Or do you let her know what you wish she would do because you love and care for her?

Our son, Keith, and his wife, Jane, pointed this out to me by the way they raise their son, Charlie. Keith showed me the difference between saying "Don't do that" and "Please be careful and safe." One is critical and the other says I love you.

Praise is the other important element. Accentuate the positive, and the negative begins to fade away. We all grow through praise and bloom with love.

Soulution of the Day

Try to accentuate the positive and eliminate the negative through loving words and actions. Notice the difference.

HUMAN KIND

Each of us inevitable; each of us limitless —
each of us with his or her right upon
the earth; each of us allowed the eternal
purports of the earth; each of us here
as divinely as any is here.

— WALT WHITMAN

ONE DAY I REALIZED that it was a lot easier for a house full of animals to get along than it was for five children. It made me think about the human family. It seems to me that it is always easier to talk about loving humankind and generalize about how we should treat each other, than it is to get along with one individual.

Why can't we see each other as representing humankind, as being of the same family, and treat each other as a reflection of ourselves? Perhaps one day we will come to realize that we are all members of the same family. Families may have their problems, but they are always safe in the knowledge of acceptance and support, regardless of their differences.

It is no coincidence that the words *human* and *kind* have been put together to form this family. Let us live what our name implies. We are one entity, humankind. And, like our bodies, to injure one part is to hurt the whole. We are a team and when one player is injured, the entire team suffers.

It is time that we look past all our external differences and realize that we are all the same color on the inside.

Soulution of the Day

Today make a conscious effort to connect the words human *and* kind.
Be aware of how this changes your behavior.

TRUE THERAPY

*If you really want to understand me,
please hear what I am not saying,
what I may never be able to say.*

— **ANONYMOUS**

IF WE WOULD ALL REALLY LISTEN to each other, we would save on therapy by seeing one another as the beautiful creations we are.

A while back, my wife and I were due to go to a wedding. Bobbie refused to go, saying, "I have nothing to wear. Nothing fits right anymore."

I replied, "Okay, dear, let's go shopping and I'll buy you a new dress." I must have said that a million times with no response.

One day, tired of trying to get her motivated to shop, I responded differently. She said, "I have nothing to wear. I am not going to the wedding."

I responded, "You are so beautiful it makes no difference what you wear. No one notices your clothing. They only see your beauty." My wife went to the wedding wearing a dress she had in the closet. I saved a lot of money, but more important, she felt good about herself.

Soulution of the Day

*Listen to what someone isn't saying today and then respond
to what they really mean.*

YOU ARE HUMAN

This above all; to thine own self be true.

— WILLIAM SHAKESPEARE

PEOPLE ENDURE CERTAIN CIRCUMSTANCES that other living things do not have to deal with: parents, educational systems, governments, and religions. Because of these factors and the way we interpret them, we often grow up feeling there is something wrong with us. There is nothing wrong with us except the fact that we are human.

When I speak at high schools, I have one of the teachers bring his or her infant son or daughter to the talk. When I hold up the baby, the auditorium full of students sighs in awe of the beautiful child. Then I point to a student, and everyone laughs. Why? What has happened to us in those few intervening years that makes us laugh at ourselves rather than revel in our beauty?

The hardest thing to do is to love ourselves and to feel free to be ourselves. Others can still guide and teach us, but we must not let them control our lives!

Soulution of the Day

Get out your baby pictures and fall in love with yourself again. You are a divine child. Act toward yourself as a loving grandparent would who is capable of unconditional love.

PRAISE

The sweetest of all sounds is praise.

— **XENOPHON**

PRAISE IS SEEN IN YOUR EYES when you look at your beloved. Praise is felt in your touch when you embrace. Praise is heard in your voice when you speak to the one you adore. Praise is about your loved one's potential and the hope you have for that person. Praise is like helium; it lifts us up above the troubles and obstacles of life.

Praise does not say you are perfect. It says I admire you and what you have accomplished and what I know you will go on to do. Praise is the food of the soul. No one survives without it.

Soulution of the Day

*Praise is like fertilizer. Sprinkle it freely,
and those you love will grow, bloom, and blossom.*

PRESCRIPTION #92

LAWS

*If the individual is to be happy,
healthy, and prosperous, he must change
from the Laws of the Mind (negative)
to the Laws of the Soul (positive).*

— HIGHLAND BEAM CLUB

WHICH EMOTIONS LEAD to a state of happiness or unhappiness? Ask yourself which are prevalent in your life right now and which ones you might be holding onto in an attempt to avoid change.

Think about these words: *fear, worry, selfishness, vanity, anger, criticism, envy, greed, hypocrisy, prejudice, jealousy,* and *hate.* Read that list a few times and be aware of the effect it has on how you are feeling. These feelings originate from the Laws of the Mind and will keep you in a state of unhappiness.

Now try these words and watch the transformation: *faith, hope, generosity, aspiration, patience, sympathy, goodness, kindness, courage, duty,* and *love.* These words come from the Laws of the Soul and will open you to happiness.

Soulution of the Day

Which laws will you follow today?

READ MY MIND

*Intuition is a spiritual faculty
and does not explain, but simply
points the way.*

— FLORENCE SCOVEL SHINN

THE OTHER DAY I wanted to groom our four cats, bathe our dog, clip their toenails, and brush their teeth. As soon as I thought about doing it, our dog went to the other end of the house to hide. Then our most fearful cat jumped off the sofa and hid under the furniture. They were able to read my thoughts. I had no equipment out and hadn't picked anyone up at that point. I was just thinking about it.

I have no doubt that we can read each other's minds and communicate without speaking. I test the animals by thinking different things as I approach them. When they are aware that I have no intention of grooming them, they lie in my path and I have to step over them. But if I walk into the room thinking about something they don't want, like a trip to the vet, they are gone. Two outdoor cats didn't show up for a week when I made a vet appointment for their annual checkup. When I canceled the appointment they showed up for breakfast the next day.

Sometimes we block our intuitive abilities and take our antennas down, because as humans we talk only in words. Animals have many ways of communicating, using sounds, images, or intuition. Like them we need to become more aware of our other sources of communication.

Soulution of the Day

Be open to listening and speaking without words.

OVERWHELM

Take your life in your own hands,
and what happens? A terrible thing:
no one to blame.

— ERICA JONG

WHEN YOU ARE FEELING OVERWHELMED, stop and ask yourself why you are feeling that way. Who created the situation that you find overwhelming? If it was someone asking for your help, why didn't you say no? If you feel overwhelmed because of all the things you have undertaken, when will you realize that you have needs too?

Becoming angry or resenting your family, co-workers, and the world in general will not solve anything. Only you can change things by accepting your humanity and asking for what you need. Remember that saying no to others is saying yes to you.

No matter what you learned growing up, there is no reason to feel guilty about caring for yourself and your needs. When you do start to take better care of yourself, you will find much more peace with the world and the people in it. Instead of blaming them for your troubles, you will realize you are the problem and you are also the solution.

Soulution of the Day

Become more aware of your needs.
Ask for the help you require, and say no when you need to.

PRESCRIPTION #95

MEANINGFUL FRUIT

The fruit of silence is prayer.
The fruit of prayer is faith.
The fruit of faith is love.
The fruit of love is service.
The fruit of service is peace.

— MOTHER TERESA

WORDS ALWAYS CARRY A DEEPER MEANING than common usage ascribes to them. When I hear the word *fruit* I think of something to eat. Yet the fruit of our labors is usually not edible, unless we are working on a farm. Likewise, the word *produce* can apply to food in a market or to what we produce through our creative efforts.

If we are to nourish ourselves we need to produce a meaningful fruit from our labor. We need to nourish not only our body but our soul and spirit as well. To not meet the needs of all will cause you to be malnourished. Often we overfeed our body when it is our spirit or soul that is starving. Insulating ourselves with fat does not give us the real nourishment we need.

Stop thinking about the material things related to the words *fruit, produce,* and *nourishment.* Instead bring the spiritual and soulful aspects of those words into your life. Choose your way of producing the fruits of your labor so that through them you nourish yourself and the world. You will never feel as fulfilled by eating a meal as you will by performing your right action.

Soulution of the Day

Do not starve your mind, body, spirit, or soul.
Discover what feeds them and make this a steady part of your diet.

STAINED GLASS

People are like a stained-glass window.
They sparkle and shine when the sun is out.

— ELISABETH KÜBLER-ROSS

MOST OF US ARE VERY CONCERNED about revealing the so-called stains on our lives. We are constantly trying to hide our scars and wrinkles with cosmetics, plastic surgery, and medications. We try a variety of other therapies both physical and psychological to remove the stains. The truth is we are hiding what makes us unique because we are afraid of being different and of being noticed.

Why do we hide our wounds when we know that everyone is wounded? Why deny what makes us unique? My teachers are those who make no effort to hide their stains, scars, and wrinkles. They step forward and are as whole as anyone I have ever met. They know their true self, the immortal, ever beautiful self.

When I meet those who are unique because of their stains, I see works of art. When we do not hide from the light by drawing our shades, all of us become stained-glass windows through which God can shine with a beautiful hue.

Soulution of the Day

Go forth into the world and like a crystal create a rainbow
with the light reflected by your life!

CHANGES

*It's never too late to become
the person you have always been.*

— JOHN KIMBROUGH

WHEN YOU WANT TO CHANGE, you may start by buying new clothes, moving, redecorating, getting a new job, cleaning out your closets, and so on. But that is not what will change *you*. Those activities only change aspects of your life. To change yourself, you must start on the inside.

I am talking about changing from the inside out. When the essential you is altered, the rest will follow. An Alcoholics Anonymous slogan is "fake it till you make it." They are not talking about dressing differently or trying to fool people but about making the effort to be the person you want to be.

By faking it and acting like the person you truly want to be, you begin the change, and will start to do the inner work. When you become different inside, it will reflect on the outside, and all will know and recognize the new you.

Soulution of the Day

*What changes would you like to make?
Decide how you want to be, work on those changes,
and act as if you are already there.*

PRESCRIPTION #98

EFFORT

*It's the constant and determined effort
that breaks down resistance,
sweeps away all obstacles.*

— CLAUDE M. BRISTOL

WHY DO YOU EXTEND YOURSELF and put extra effort into certain tasks? Is it the desire for personal gain or reward that keeps you working overtime? What motivates you to really perform work of the highest quality and put in the effort needed to achieve your desired results?

I hope the answers to those questions are not related only to extrinsic and material things but to an effort to do what is right as well. We are all here to work for what is right. Through our efforts we can create a better world. When we start doing the right things for the right reasons, we will create the right world.

Soulution of the Day

*What are you willing to put out the effort for?
Do as the marines say in their training motto and
"Choose the difficult right over the easy wrong."*

I USED TO WORRY

Do not dwell in the past,
do not dream of the future, concentrate the
mind on the present moment.

— BUDDHA

LAST NIGHT I WAS TALKING ON THE PHONE to our daughter, Carolyn, and she said, "I used to worry about death, but now I have kids!" I laughed because now that she has two sons who are very young, ages two and one, she has no time to worry about things that might happen. She is too busy taking care of her loved ones in the reality of the moment.

Time and worry are often related to each other. We usually worry about events that are in the past or future. When we have time to worry about our difficulties — what may happen or what has happened — our fears and disappointments become our focus. However, if we occupy ourselves with living and focusing in the present, as animals and infants do, our fears and worries lessen.

It has been shown that most of what we worry about never comes to be. And I don't know of any problem that was solved by worrying about it. So take care of what the world needs *now:* love, sweet love. If you come from a place of love, you will be able to deal with anything that happens.

Soulution of the Day

Taking care of what needs doing now
leaves little time for fear and worry.

TIME OUT

The time to relax is when
you don't have time for it.

— JIM GOODWIN AND SYDNEY J. HARRIS

TODAY WAS QUIET AND PEACEFUL. I wasn't going anywhere. I was just being me. And it felt good to be me. That's a change. The old me would have been too busy doing things, never even making time for a nap.

Often we run around with our many to-do lists and never have the time to even get to know ourselves. Perhaps if we took the time for inner quiet, a short nap, or for doing nothing, we would accomplish a great deal more.

Soulution of the Day

Do nothing to accomplish everything.
Put a nap and quiet time at the top of your list today.
Don't wait for a physical affliction to force you to change your schedule.

COOPERATION

*Behold how good and how pleasant it is
for brethren to dwell together in unity!*

— PSALM 133:1

ON MY FIRST VISIT TO HEAVEN as an outside consultant to the Board of Directors, I was surprised to see so many angels with only one wing. I asked one of the angels why he wasn't healed of his affliction. He didn't answer but simply turned and embraced another one-winged angel, and off they flew. It was so beautiful to see how what we as humans view as an affliction could be turned into a blessing, with a little cooperation.

I was struck by the thought of what humankind could achieve if we all embraced each other and worked together. Imagine a world where we all cooperate with each other; then all our actions would reflect the work of angels.

Soulution of the Day

*When we all learn to work together in harmony,
we will be uplifted by our acts and notice our feet
are no longer touching the ground.*

PARTNERS IN CRIME

Kill with kindness.

— Sixteenth-century proverb

THE OTHER DAY someone saw me without my wife and asked where my "partner in crime" was. The term struck me because we use it to suggest two people working closely together. Fortunately, most of the time it is not related to doing anything criminal but something beneficial, and it suggests an enviable closeness.

I like to think that my wife and I are partners in crime using love and laughter to wipe out the enemy. Our weapons don't hurt anyone and can be used freely when we see an act that hurts someone. We step forward to kill the offenders with kindness or torment them with tenderness. It is not an accident when we say love thine enemies; it is one way of obliterating them.

Perhaps we need to come up with a new partnership title, like partners in crime obliteration. We would threaten to love everybody and see what effect that would have.

Soulution of the Day

*Who could be your partner in crime to help make this world
a more loving and peaceful place?*

EXORCISE REGULARLY

One of the greatest moments in anybody's developing experience is when he no longer tries to hide from himself, but determines to get acquainted with himself as he really is.

— NORMAN VINCENT PEALE

EXORCISE! No, that is not misspelled, just good advice! I am all for regular exercise, and I make sure I get some myself, but I think it is more important to exorcise daily. Why not schedule your exercise and exorcise at the same time, since the mind and body are a unit?

Think of the distressing things in your life you would like to be free of, the bad habits, behavior patterns, and "devilish" activities that you know are injuring you and others. Well, exorcise them!

One of the main reasons I run away from home every day — I mean, why I go jogging every day — is to be alone with my thoughts. Sometimes our dog accompanies me, but he knows not to interrupt me.

My ritual includes thinking about the things I am grateful for, no matter how difficult life may be at the moment. Next, I confess to myself all the things I don't like about my behavior, especially toward those whom I may have hurt. At this point I truly work on exorcising these behaviors and contemplate how I plan to change and become the person I want to be. I rehearse in my mind how I will do this. I accept that I am part of the problem and that I am only human. After all, human beings are not as complete as other animals are. So I have some work to do, exorcising my human fallibility and becoming more like Lassie.

Soulution of the Day

Stop making excuses and start exorcising today! Then go on to pray for, or send blessings to, all the people in your life. Ask to achieve peace of mind and for the strength to become a loving human being.

KIDS: DEVILS OR ANGELS

Actions speak louder than words.

— MARK TWAIN

SINCE KIDS DON'T LISTEN a lot of the time anyway, don't worry too much about what you say. But, worry a lot about what you do.

I'll always remember an interaction I had with our son Keith many years ago. He is one of the twins and was an angel as a child. Therefore, he had the bedroom at the end of the hall because we didn't have to worry about him or what he was doing when his door was shut.

At the time his brother Jeffrey was driving us nuts. So his bedroom was right there in plain view at all times, and occasionally I took the door off the hinges to be sure he would get up and go to school on time.

One day Keith came to me and said, "I don't get 20 percent of your time."

"What do you mean?" I responded.

Keith said, "You have five children, and we should each get 20 percent."

"Well," I said, "your brother is driving us crazy, so he gets 40 percent."

I learned from this interaction with my son that the "angels" in your life need to know you care for and love them too. They think they are at the end of the hall because you don't love them as much, while the "devils" know you love them because they get most of your attention.

Soulution of the Day

Don't use the excuse "the devil made me do it!"
Pay close attention to how your actions are perceived by your kids.

ENDANGERED SPECIES

We are becoming something less
than we have ever been — aliens to each
other and adversaries to Creation's creatures.

— DEIRDRE LUZWICK

WHEN YOU SEE the words *endangered species,* do you ever stop and think that they could be referring to you? We are an endangered species too. We are the biggest danger to ourselves and to our planet. Too often the only thing that turns people's behavior around is a brush with death and their acceptance of their mortality.

Let us hope that we do not have to wait until life on this planet has almost vanished before we become one family, intent on preserving life. Until then, it is too easy to say one species is more important than another, making it all right to kill owls, trees, whales, people of certain religions and nationalities, and those of other races. We all need to make love, not war. Love-making leads to creation, and war to destruction.

Let us prove that Oscar Wilde's words, "I sometimes think that God, in creating man, somewhat overestimated His abilities," do not predict the future.

Soulution of the Day

We are all in this together and have to
stop separating ourselves from each other.

FARMS AND CITIES

*Man's heart away
from nature becomes hard.*

— STANDING BEAR

*I fly over the farmlands...
An abstract artist painted them:
Beautiful lines, curves, greens,
Browns, beauty.
Creation lies beneath me.
The homes fit between the lines,
But are lost in the beauty of the earth.
I fly over the city...
Straight lines, squares, boxes, lined up like soldiers.
It hurts my eyes to see what we have done
Nature has no room.
Please scatter the houses
And make room for the earth
To blossom.*

Soulution of the Day

Do your part to keep the earth blossoming.

WHOLE LIFE POLICY

Men are only as great as they are kind.

— ELBERT HUBBARD

YOU CANNOT BUY AN INSURANCE POLICY to guarantee that you will live a whole and complete life. A complete life is not about time, but about our actions...particularly our acts of kindness.

One of my favorite quotes, from Stephen Grellet, that I try to live by is "I expect to pass through the world but once. Any good therefore that I can do, or any kindness that I can show to my fellow creature, let me do it now. Let me not defer or neglect it, for I shall not pass this way again." This quote says it all.

If you want to live a complete life, then find a way to share kindness. If you wonder who, when, and how to help, just look at the person in front of you. Do for her what she needs done, now.

Soulution of the Day

Perform the acts of kindness we all came here to do.

DON'T WORRY ABOUT NOTHING

Worry is a sustained form of fear caused by indecision.

— BRIAN TRACY

WHEN YOU WORRY ABOUT NOTHING, you are worrying about all the things that will probably never happen but are a part of your unhealthy fantasizing. Does worrying solve anything or eradicate the problem? No. Does it lead to problems for the person worrying? Yes.

When you worry about something, you still are not solving the problem by worrying. You have to get it through your head that worry, anxiety, unrest, panic, and fear of the future does not make the problem go away.

What will make the problem go away? Once we determine the source of our worries we can begin to deal with them in a positive way. The basis for most, if not all of these worries, is fear. Dr. Gerald Jampolsky states in his book *Love Is Letting Go of Fear* that we come either from a place of love or one of fear, and love is the only reality there is. He goes on to say, "Fear always distorts our perception and confuses us as to what is going on. Love is the total absence of fear...love, then, is really everything that is of value and fear can offer us nothing because it is nothing."

Soulution of the Day

Do not worry about anything.
It doesn't pay or make sense.

TOLL TAKERS

*You have not fulfilled every duty,
unless you have fulfilled that of
being pleasant.*

— CHARLES BUXTON

A WHILE AGO I drove from New York to Maine and was impressed by the difference in the attitude and character of the toll takers. For some, their work was taking a toll on them.

In New York the music coming out of the booth was loud and fast, and it was a pleasure to leave the sound. The toll taker didn't relate to me or make eye contact. They handed me the change, and away I drove.

I usually like to interact and say things like, "How can I help you?" One of the times I asked that question, the toll taker responded by asking me to get out of my car, take over for her, and let her drive off. We had a good laugh. Since I was reimbursed with a laugh, this toll stop didn't cost me anything. In Maine the music was soft, slow, and soothing. I didn't mind waiting for my change. I noticed the toll taker was more interested in talking to me and was withholding my change so he and I could go on speaking. He enjoyed my company, and I his. Again there was a refund on the toll.

Soulution of the Day

Don't let life take its toll; live a life that reimburses you.

RULES AND REGULATIONS

There are two worlds: the world that we can measure with line and rule, and the world we feel with our hearts and imagination.

— LEIGH HUNT

THE MORE RULES AND REGULATIONS we create, the more we separate ourselves from each other. Once we label someone as a troublemaker or a sinner, the problems start. When we judge people by a list of society's words, we are in big trouble.

None of us is perfect. We are all learning. When I have problems with our children, I don't label them as sinners for not honoring their parents. I ask them why they are treating me this way. If I start labeling them, I become the problem because now I am blaming the children and elevating myself above them. But if I come from my heart and use my imagination to respond, it leaves room for healing.

When I stop responding with judgment as a parent or human being, other people seem nicer and are no longer a problem either. So measure others with your heart and let the magic happen. Live in the world of imagination and dreams, and not in the world of rules and regulations.

Soulution of the Day

For today, don't be or create a problem. Solve one instead.

WISDOM
OF THE AGED

The question is not whether
we will die, but how we will live.

— JOAN BORYSENKO

TODAY'S PAPER contains an article about a man who died at age one hundred and ten. A short time before his death, a researcher at Yale asked him how he avoided falling down. He said, "I watch where I am going." Then the doctor asked his advice on how to live a long life. The man responded, "Be kind to people. Give in sometimes and help people when you can."

I find advice from the aged is never about what vegetable to eat or how often to exercise. It is about enjoying life and people. It is about being here to love, laugh, serve, and to live fully. They often say things like, "We're too busy to die," and that the only thing they fear is driving on the parkway at night.

Just before I attended a conference on aging, I asked my ninety-seven-year-old, quadriplegic father-in-law his advice on the topic. Several years earlier, wearing new bifocals, he had fallen off his porch and seriously injured his spinal cord. He responded, "Tell them to fall on something soft." A few days later he told me this advice didn't always work. It seems while he was in therapy, they stood him up and he fell over on his wife and broke her leg. "So tell them to just fall *up*," he said.

I laughed but later realized he was telling me something important. When the body becomes tired and can no longer serve, each day becomes work. When you leave this earth, hopefully you will fall *up*. That's what my father-in-law did quietly one evening.

Soulution of the Day

Be kind, give in sometimes, and help others.

TREASURE CHEST

From you I have learned so many things,
but in truth they won't be of much use,
for when I keep them within
this suitcase, unhappily shall I be dying.

— GABRIEL GARCÍA MÁRQUEZ

THINK OF ALL THE THINGS you experience that you lock up inside yourself. I always think of it as closing the lid, like when you pack your suitcase full and then close and lock the lid. Sometimes we do that with our lives and travel the road of life with everything packed tightly inside of us. In the process, we destroy the beauty of the journey.

I have learned to take the lid off and let out what is within me. I want my heart to live in a treasure chest and not a suitcase of discarded events. Yes, there may have been events that wounded me, but I have learned you can't heal what you bury within yourself, and it will just go on wounding you at a deeper level of being.

When he learns he is dying of cancer, Márquez, whom I quoted above, goes on to say many things in his good-bye letter. This Nobel Prize–winning author writes, "I would write my hate on ice, and wait for the sun to show...and how I would enjoy a good chocolate ice cream. I have learned that everyone wants to live on the peak of the mountain, without knowing that real happiness is in how it is scaled."

Soulution of the Day

Travel with a light heart and a treasure chest full of love,
and your journey will be much easier.

POOR SPELLERS OR POWERFUL MESSAGES?

Intuition is the deepest wisdom of the soul.
— JEFFREY MISHLOVE

ONE DAY I WAS TYPING an email to our daughter, Carolyn, and accidentally wrote the word *lioving*. I didn't correct it because I thought it was a wonderful new word that contained great meaning. Did I mean to type *living* or *loving*? I think *lioving* means both. So my daughter and I now have a word that expresses what we were created to experience despite life's difficulties.

I continued to type because I wanted to compliment our daughter on something that she had done for her children. I intended to type *good* work — but instead I typed *godd* work. I liked that word too and left it! If we do *godd* work we are doing good work in our Creator's name.

It's nice to make these kinds of illuminating spelling errors. But then are they really errors? Freud and Jung would tell us otherwise! Perhaps these unconscious mistakes are to remind us to listen to our inner voice and follow its therapeutic directions.

Soulution of the Day

*At times we need to think less and feel more
by letting our intuitive wisdom come into play.*

PRAY FOR ME

If you do not know what to pray for, recite
the alphabet and let God create the prayer.

— ANONYMOUS

IF I ASKED YOU what I could pray for for you, what would you answer? Stop and think about your answer. Most people ask for prayers relating to personal needs and desires: health, wealth, peace of mind, a new job, and whatever poses a problem in their life at the moment.

While visiting my ninety-five-year-old mother-in-law, who was having a tough day at the nursing home, I asked her, "What can I pray for, for you?" I was trying to let her vent her anger and needs. I was expecting her to say pray for a nurse to come, better food, someone to change my bed, or something similar.

She paused for a moment and said, "World peace."

Needless to say, I shall never forget that moment and the respect I felt for her. She had transcended herself and her needs. How many of us will reach that point in our lives?

Soulution of the Day

What can I pray for, for you, today?
Give some thought to what you are asking for.
While personal prayers ease our life's journey,
prayers for the greater good of our fellow human beings
enhance our lives in untold measures.

FAIL SUCCESSFULLY

*You can be discouraged by failure —
or you can learn from it.*

— T. J. WATSON

YOU CAN SEE FAILURE as a reason to stop what you are doing, or you can ask yourself why you failed and then learn from your mistakes. Mistakes can be a valuable part of life's curriculum.

You would do well to fail frequently so you can learn a great deal more than someone who is afraid to fail and therefore takes little risk. If you have passion for what you are doing and aim high, good things will happen even if it takes a lot of failing to accomplish them.

Accidents, failures, and mistakes can often lead us to our greatest successes and open us to our true interests. For instance, say you have a project you want to complete but you need more knowledge of the subject. So you take an evening course at a local college. You walk into the wrong class and become so interested in the subject that it changes your life.

Soulution of the Day

*An "F" in the subject of life doesn't just stand for failure.
It can also stand for fun, flow, find, finish — and more.*

COMPLAINTS

A man is responsible for his choice
of attention and must accept
the consequences.

— W. H. AUDEN

SINCE WE ALL SPEND TIME complaining, we must have much in common. What is unique is how each person finds a solution to his or her problems.

The answers are within us, and that is the last place many of us ever look. It is so much easier to find a solution "out there" or to have things solved by someone else. Then you can sit home safe and secure with the problems you are comfortable with. Why go searching for answers? Why feel anything or see the truth?

Another thing we have in common with one another is the fear of change. But change is inevitable, while growth is optional. When we are willing to reach into the depths of our souls, we will find the answer. The voice of the cosmos speaks in symbols and not rational language. The symbols are hidden within each of us. Your solutions lie where you fear to go, obscured by your shadow.

Soulution of the Day

Go within and you will never come up empty-handed.

MOVIES OF YOUR MIND

Imagination is more powerful than knowledge.

— ALBERT EINSTEIN

YOUR LIFE IS CREATED by the movies of your mind. What you picture, your body experiences and your life becomes. You are a character playing a role, but who wrote the script and who is directing the show?

What you imagine and picture should not be dictated and scripted by others. This is your movie, your show, and don't let them tell you how it should be performed or how long it has to play. Most of all, don't let anyone drop the curtain on you until you say the show is over.

Sit down, picture what you want, and write out the script. Then give a copy to everyone who is playing a part in the movie of your life. If they can't play their part, replace them with understudies who do care and believe in you and your show.

Soulution of the Day

Remember, you are the director of the movies of your mind.

MAGNETS

*People of opposing views often
march under the same banner.*

— WILLI RITSCHARD

MAGNETS ARE INTERESTING THINGS. Opposites attract, and likes repel. Their qualities remind me of people. Think about the people in your life you feel uncomfortable with and those you feel attracted to. They are telling you something about yourself.

When someone shows a side of you that you are not comfortable with, you repel them because they confront you with aspects of your shadow that you want to deny. On the other hand, when someone exemplifies the qualities you wish you possessed, you are attracted to them. When people compliment me, I always tell them they are describing themselves, because if those qualities weren't in them they wouldn't find them in me.

When they criticize me, I know they are also speaking about themselves, and I have learned to stop explaining and making excuses, because the problem isn't me. Now I just say, "Thank you, I love you" and let them become demagnetized.

Soulution of the Day

Love and be attracted by love and demagnetize those who criticize you.

ROAD RAGE

*Anger will never disappear so long as
thoughts of resentment are cherished in
the mind. Anger will disappear just as soon
as thoughts of resentment are forgotten.*

— BUDDHA

ROAD RAGE has become prevalent in today's society. With all the daily stressors, people build up anger until it becomes resentment. They hold it within until it becomes bitterness, then hatred, until one day on the way home "some idiot" doesn't move when the light turns green and boom, they explode. It isn't the other driver they are responding to, it is all the built-up anger stored within. When it releases, it can injure them and perhaps others who are near at the time.

One day in my car I saw a bumper sticker that said, "Honk if you love Jesus." I honked, and the guy gave me the finger! Maybe it wasn't his car. When I run into road rage I just shout, "I love you" at the people involved. That really sets them off because no one has ever been that mean to them before. It invariably gets them to drive away saying things I am sure I don't need or want to hear.

I was cruel one day when a young man behind me was honking and cursing. A nearby policeman did not help me when I asked him to speak to the young man. So I went over and said to him, "I am sorry your parents don't love you, but I want you to know I love you." He made a U-turn and sped away. Our children tell me I am lucky he didn't shoot me.

Soulution of the Day

*We all need to find responsible ways to release our anger
and prevent it from building up into a case of road rage.*

BE KIND TO THE WOUNDED

*In love's service only the
wounded soldier can serve.*

— THORNTON WILDER

MANY YEARS AGO, when I was working as a counselor at a day camp, I saw a boy in my group emptying his locker one Friday afternoon. I didn't know why he was taking everything home, but before I could ask, a group of boys came over and started teasing him. In a flash they scattered his things all over the ground. I ran over to help him. Afterward I asked him where he lived. When it turned out he lived near my house I offered him a ride home. He accepted, and the head of the camp had no objections, so off we went. He was awkward and uncoordinated and no one ever wanted him on their team, so I was surprised at how bright and humorous his conversation was on the way home.

I invited him to come to the game I was going to be in the next day, and to make a long story short, we became close friends. We drove home together each day, and I'd always pick him for my teams at camp.

Years later I was invited to the boy's graduation from high school. He was the valedictorian and very different from the chubby young man I had known. He spoke of the day we had met and said, "I was emptying my locker because I was planning to commit suicide and didn't want my parents to have to go through the emotional strain of picking up my things. Then someone intervened to help me. Never underestimate the power of your actions."

Soulution of the Day

*Remember, we are all wounded. Be an angel and when someone
is having trouble with their wings, lift them up. You will be uplifted too.*

PRESCRIPTION #121

WHERE'S HOME

*Show me a man who cares no more
for one place than another and I will
show you in that same person one who
loves nothing but himself.*

— ROBERT SOUTHEY

AS I STEPPED OFF THE PLANE after a recent trip, someone asked me, "Are you home yet?"

I said, "Of course. This is my planet."

What do you think of as home? Whether it is one acre or a whole continent, do you treat your homeland differently than the homeland of others? Or are all homelands sacred to you?

In actuality, you are home everywhere on this planet. We all share the furnishings, the environment, and the air we breathe and re-breathe. Treat it all like your home and care for it so that your descendants, of whatever blood relationship, race, religion, or nationality, can live here in the years to come.

If we feel at home with those around us, we will create a home for the future. But if we build fences, fight with our neighbors, intrude on them, and damage their property, we will all lose our homes some day.

Soulution of the Day

*Are you home yet? Of course you are; this is your planet!
So create a home for everyone by landscaping your life
for the pleasure of all to see.*

GETTING TO KNOW YOU

The greatest of faults is to be conscious of none.
— THOMAS CARLYLE

GETTING TO KNOW YOURSELF BETTER takes courage. It is far easier to hide behind a mask than to see yourself as you really are. There are many who think they are perfect and need not change, who think they're the center of the universe, and they have a problem.

If you wish to know yourself and change for the better, you need to accept your inadequacies, fears, weaknesses, mistakes, and more. If you need others present constantly to entertain and distract you, then you are afraid to be still and know yourself.

So spend some time being totally alone and see how you feel. If you are comfortable, then I would say you are in the process of knowing yourself. Knowing yourself means being willing to be with yourself. Once you can do that, the frantic search for distraction and escape will stop ruling your life and you can choose to fill your life with the things that bring you joy.

Soulution of the Day

*Even if it feels uncomfortable, go away with yourself
and spend some time together getting to know yourself.
You may find that you are great company.*

XOXOXOXO

Hugging closes the door to hate.
Kissing opens the door to love.

— TONY DAVIS

MY WIFE AND DAUGHTER sometimes use symbols to convey their love to me. An *X* is a kiss, and an *O* is a hug. When Carolyn sends me an email she always sends hugs and kisses. When I am traveling alone, my wife, Bobbie, sneaks notes into my luggage so I can find them as I travel. She draws her face and sketches all the pets we have and sends me hugs and love. The note ends with, "We love you. Call us. XOXOXOXO."

I have saved them all, and they are around the house both framed and in nooks and crannies where I will be searching at some time. There is nothing as wonderful, especially when I'm having a bad day, as finding one of those notes. They always bring a smile to my face.

I am writing this on what has been a difficult day. We had a big snowstorm today, and I drove my wife to a doctor's appointment. It turns out we were there on the wrong day and the doctor wasn't in. It did not leave me with a good feeling. I came home and saw one of the special notes on the wall with the XOXOXOXO on it, and all was forgiven.

Soulution of the Day

Make notes with pictures of all the creatures in your home.
Add XOXOXOXO and place them in your loved ones' drawers,
socks, lunches, and so on. Place them all over your house so you can find
them too, and remember how good hugs and kisses feel.

FACE VALUE

*The chief value of money lies
in the fact that one lives in a world in
which it is overestimated.*

— H. L. MENCKEN

ONE OF OUR SONS was upset when he built a house and didn't make a profit selling it. I was proud of what he had done. I told him he had created something that would give me and others pleasure every time we drove past it. The pleasure I derived was from what he created and the quality of his work. It was not related to how much money he made or lost. I honor his work because of what he put into it and not the sale price.

Do you build and work only to make money, or do you also value creating something? Everything has its results, and the long-term results are ultimately not in the dollar sign but in the life sign.

Soulution of the Day

*To see your true worth, see the value in what you do
or create beyond its material compensation.*

PAINTING

Buy a paint box and have a try.
— WINSTON CHURCHILL

I ENJOYED PAINTING as a child and resumed it as an adult when I was in emotional turmoil working as a surgeon and needed to be healed. Involving myself and our children in painting took away all the pain and restored me. These words of Winston Churchill about painting say it all: "I know of nothing which, without exhausting the body, more entirely absorbs the mind. Whatever the worries of the hour or the threats of the future, once the picture has begun to flow there is no room for them in the mental screen."

Not only does painting not exhaust you, it energizes you. You do not have to be a Picasso or van Gogh to enjoy creating. When you begin to paint, you see the beauty of nature as well as the beauty of your work of art. The world will never look the same after you decide to paint.

My paintings hang in our home and in the homes of our family. I have painted a portrait of my parents that hangs in their home. They did not know I had painted it from photographs. I took them to the gallery where it was being displayed in a show, and they were thrilled to see themselves as a work of art. I have done many portraits of our children and grandchildren, and they remind me of the passage of time as I look on their young faces displayed in our home.

Soulution of the Day

Buy a paint box, or borrow your child's, and have a try.

TOO LATE?

*You cannot do a kindness too soon,
for you never know how soon
it will be too late.*

— RALPH WALDO EMERSON

A FAMOUS PAINTING portrays a dying child, his parents, and the doctor in a one-room cabin. When I've asked other doctors a multiple-choice question about what the painting should be named, many say "Too Late." Why? Because they see the doctor, chin in hand, thinking about what he could possibly do that might help the child, who is beyond help. The parents are seen grieving in the background.

But it isn't too late, because the doctor could be helping the parents to survive their loss. Most of us are poorly prepared for loss. We deny it. As children, we are often not allowed to attend funerals or discuss death. Our pets die and are immediately replaced.

We need to remember that it is never too late to help one another, and never too late to deal with our feelings. Burying our losses in the ground or in our bodies doesn't do the trick. So help the living, and don't save the flowers for the grave.

Soulution of the Day

*As long as there is someone who needs your help,
it is never too late to reach out.*

NOURISHMENT

What you need to sustain you
does not need to be chewed to be digested.

— KNUTE SHMEDLEY

WHAT NOURISHES ME is not food alone. It does appease my hunger and restore my energy. What feeds me is the love displayed by those who are willing to prepare a meal for me. The love that goes into the preparation is tasted in every bite. Their desire and intention alter the food and make its effects transcend mere nutritive and caloric values.

What nourishes us all are relationships, love, joy, and all the good feelings we are capable of experiencing. We need to be touched physically and emotionally to be nourished. The untouched child does not thrive; the touched child fed the same amount as an untouched one gains weight 50 percent faster.

We need to designate touch and love as essential vitamins and minerals for our survival. They need to be a part of the diet pyramid. Without them, what enters us does not become metabolized and used to create life. Learn to ingest what you need. Each person's diet may vary. Find your unique form of nourishment.

Soulution of the Day

Seek nourishment and do not starve your body or your life spirit.

SMILE

Smile; it's free therapy.
— DOUG HORTON

IF WE CAN'T SMILE, how will we survive? But is the smile real or put on to make others happy? Maybe the person smiling feels anything but the desire to smile. I see this in the drawings seriously ill people do. They will draw a big smile on the face of the main character, even though they have a life-threatening illness and to quote one patient "a husband who's never there when you need him."

Or ask someone, "How are you?" He will almost always answer, "Fine," even if his house has just burned down! When I answer, "Better" when asked the above question people always want to know what's wrong. I say, "Nothing's wrong. I'm just getting better."

I refuse to stop smiling. I find things to smile about because I know life is an adventure and Lord knows what is coming tomorrow. I don't think anyone would come back from their grave and say, "Get serious." But I do think they would come back and say, "Lighten up." So be a little crazy and smile. Get better at it.

Soulution of the Day

As Woody Allen said, "Life is full of miserableness, loneliness, unhappiness, and suffering. And it's all over much too quickly."
So let a smile be your umbrella and protect you from the rain of despair.

GET COMFORTABLE

A man cannot be comfortable
without his own approval.

— MARK TWAIN

WHEN WILL YOU BE COMFORTABLE with your life? When you can impress others with all the material things you have accumulated and how expensive they are? No, having an expensive chair to recline in will not quiet your mind and allow you to be comfortable. You will never be comfortable while you are concerned with what any other person on this planet thinks about you.

Comfort only comes when you are able to love and accept yourself and the world as it is. When you accept yourself, you are no longer vulnerable and can enjoy stepping out into the world and taking chances. You are not worried about the grade you receive because you are enjoying the challenge of the course you take.

As long as you think about whether you said the right thing, are wearing the right clothes, served the right meal, did a good job, bought the right car and home, you will never be comfortable.

Soulution of the Day

Stop worrying and caring about what is right
in the eyes of others and get comfortable with yourself.

ANGELIC
CONSPIRATORS ™

Dogs are angelic conspirators that know
no boundaries and will stop at nothing
to bring you abundant love and happiness.

— JOANN MARIE DONAHUE

WHAT DO YOU CONSPIRE to create or do? What gives your life meaning? Do you arise each day wondering how you can do the work of angels, or do you awaken wondering what you can do for your own sake?

Dogs are different; they are always doing the work of angels. The word *angel* means "messenger." The message of dogs is about love and relationships. Dogs make their needs known and can be a bit annoying at dinnertime. But their requests come from their hearts, and they always respond to our love and needs.

Think about your choices and conspire to love. Imagine sending a message of love to someone who truly needs it or wouldn't ever expect one from you. Be an angel, and when you awaken every day, secretly conspire to do an angelic deed.

Soulution of the Day

Eventually your secret will be discovered, and when it is,
develop a team of angelic co-conspirators.

BEAUTY

*One's attractiveness is not defined
so much by appearance as in how another
person feels in his or her presence, or absence.*

— JOHN KIMBROUGH

ONE DAY I WENT TO THE HOME of one of my support group members. She had cancer of the tongue, and owing to her disease and treatment, her tongue was swollen and protruded from her mouth. Her head, face, and neck were swollen with fluid, and to see out of one eye she had to keep her head tilted.

Her appearance and the odor of her bedroom made me immediately think about how quickly I could make an excuse for leaving without offending her. While I was thinking she wrote a note and handed it to me. I wrote an answer and handed it back. She wrote again and handed her note to me. It said, "You don't need to write notes, you can talk."

I found myself laughing and was touched by her ability to have humor even in her condition. She became beautiful in that moment. I laughed and embraced her, and two hours later was interrupted by a call from my wife about a meeting I was expected at. I was so sorry to have to leave one of the most beautiful women I had ever known.

Soulution of the Day

If you want to find beauty, look beneath the surface.

WEAR LIFE LOOSELY

The Law of Detachment says that in order to acquire anything in the physical universe, you have to relinquish your attachment to it.

— DEEPAK CHOPRA,
THE SEVEN SPIRITUAL LAWS OF SUCCESS

IF WE SIMPLY SAW LIFE as a loose garment, something we drape around ourselves but are not firmly attached to, we would find it easier to live. I feel more comfortable living this way, as if life were something I could easily slip out of at any moment. It seems to help me focus on the important things instead of the details that mean little.

How do you want to spend your life; getting all dressed up or just wrapping yourself loosely in a comfortable garment? I don't want to waste time getting ready. I want to be free to move and live and enjoy life. I find that everything I need comes to me when I live with this sense of detachment.

Soulution of the Day

Make sure you have a comfortable fit when you dress for life.

PRACTICE MAKES PERFECT

A day will never be any more than what you make of it. Practice being a "doer."

— Josh S. Hinds

MANY YEARS AGO I attended Colgate College. I had grown up in New York City but loved the lakes and ocean where my family had gone on vacations. At Colgate I saw a sign for tryouts for the swim team. I had never seen a swim meet, never practiced swimming, but I liked the water, so I showed up.

The first thing I had to do was to dive into the pool and swim fifty yards, two lengths of the pool, as fast as I could. I had never swum in a pool and had always swum with my eyes closed. I dove in, closed my eyes, made a right turn, and swam right into the wall right in front of the coach and his staff. They stared at me dumbfounded.

Later when I looked back at this incident, what I admired most about the coach was that he didn't say, "That's it; get dressed and go." He just stared at me and then let me climb out of the pool and try again with my eyes open. This time, I did make it up and back in the pool. Of course, I was very slow, but nobody said, "Don't come to practice" or, "You can't participate." So every day I returned and practiced my swimming. My skills improved dramatically — I was even voted the most improved!

Today I know the importance of showing up and the value of practicing to become someone and to get somewhere.

Soulution of the Day

Take the time to practice the skills and abilities you want to attain.

PRESCRIPTION #134

CREATION

*You must be the change
you wish to see in the world.*

— MOHANDAS GANDHI

YOU ARE ALL CREATORS. You awaken each morning with the potential to change the world. You breathe, you talk, you eat, and you sleep. You are a creator, whether you like it or not. You can choose what you will create: life or death, love or hate. For some it is frightening to wake up to life. They continue to sleep in fear of creation. They do not realize they are creating — nothing.

Soulution of the Day

*Be an artist and create something today.
Whether it is physical or spiritual matters little,
but the process of creating will matter a lot.*

DON'T DO IT MY WAY

Live for something, have a purpose,
and that purpose keep in view;
drifting like a helmless vessel,
thou cans't ne'er to life be true.

— ROBERT WHITAKER,
LIVE FOR SOMETHING

WHILE IN A RESTAURANT, Joseph Campbell heard a man seated at a nearby table telling his child how to behave and eat. The man's wife interrupted him: "Why don't you let him do what he wants to do?" He replied, "Because I've never done anything I wanted to do in my life." Campbell said this conversation reminded him of a page out of the book *Babbitt* by Sinclair Lewis. The story tells of a father who takes his soon-to-be-married son aside for a talk. Much to the family's dismay, the son has decided to forego college, get married, and go to work. The father tells his son that he is not happy with his son's choice but that he wants him to live his own life and will therefore accept his decision. He then confesses, "Don't tell your mother this, but I have never done anything I wanted to do in my life, and I want things to be different for you." Then the father, with his arm around his son, leads them back to face the family.

I copied the page from *Babbitt* and had each of our children read it because I want them to live their own lives. I am interested in their happiness and not their specific professions. None of them are physicians, but all of them care about people. I am amazed at the things they have done and their varied interests. They have given me experiences and opportunities to learn that I never would have had if I had made them do what I wanted them to do.

I want them to live in their world, not mine, and then it becomes our world.

Soulution of the Day

Don't wait to give yourself permission to live your unique life.
Then you can say, like Frank Sinatra, "I did it my way."

PRECIOUS STONES

*We grow neither better nor worse
as we get old, but more like ourselves.*

— MAY L. BECKER

ONE MORNING I was walking along the riverbank. Each pebble I saw had chiseled on its face the years, months, and days it had lived. What had happened along this shore? My perception of the crevices and scars on the pebbles was that they added to the beauty and uniqueness of each stone.

I wondered if my face showed the weathering of time. Maybe that's the problem; perhaps we spend too much time focusing on our scars and blemishes and should instead view the true essence of ourselves — the precious stones.

Soulution of the Day

*Life may have left its marks on you,
but work toward polishing your inner beauty for an outer glow.*

SUPPORT

The ultimate measure of a man
is not where he stands in moments of comfort
and convenience, but where he stands
at times of challenge and controversy.

— MARTIN LUTHER KING JR.

YOUR LIFE IS WHIRLING AROUND YOU, and you feel dizzy and ready to fall. Now is the time to look for support. Find some firm ground to stand on, and then reach out and ask others to stand beside you to help maintain your balance.

When you were a child and whirled around a post you kept a firm grip on it so that no matter how fast you were going or many times you circled, you had support and did not fall. Remember that in your life; get a firm grip and then start whirling.

Your support post can be many different things or people. Once it is in place, you will be ready for whatever may throw you off balance. So be sure it's anchored well and that you are firmly supported by the people in your life.

Soulution of the Day

Get a grip and enjoy the merry-go-round of life.

TRY THE CHEMOTHERAPY OF LOVE

*Love is the medicine for the sickness
of the world; a prescription often given,
too rarely taken.*

— DR. KARL MENNINGER

WE ARE AWESOME CREATIONS, intricately designed and interacting in incredible ways so that our organism can survive. Yet we are constantly putting chemicals into our bodies to alter how we feel or to treat some condition we are not happy about. But what is the greatest therapy available? What is the most potent chemotherapeutic treatment ever devised? The answer is *love.*

It is the vital ingredient in the treatment of every malady and changes us in ways that no other external treatments can. It enhances our growth and development, lifts our spirits, and turns our fears of rejection into positive motivation. We literally do not grow and will even die if no one loves or touches us. Lack of love leads to self-destruction, addictions, and illnesses in every species tested. Life-sustaining measures may be taken, but without love, the most important ingredient is missing.

Soulution of the Day

*Dose yourselves with love regularly and serve others from your supply.
Dispense it with impunity because you cannot overdose,
will never run out, and there are no adverse side effects.*

PRESCRIPTION #139

FEELINGS

*If you do not bring forth what is within
you, what you do not bring forth will
destroy you. If you bring forth what is
within you, what you bring forth
will save you.*

— GOSPEL OF SAINT THOMAS

MY SON ORGANIZED A BAND when he was young. One of the songs they often played was "Feelings." I loved the song then, and it still means a lot to me now.

As far back as one can go in our history, people have written about the importance of feelings. On a personal level we know how feelings drive us to do things, from numbing ourselves when we can't handle a situation to performing acts of great courage or destruction when we're motivated by them.

I've also heard people say that while learning to think, they almost forgot how to feel. Our training and instruction does not teach us how to use our feelings properly. Feelings are meant to protect and guide us; they are not something to be obliterated. We destroy ourselves when we stop feeling. If you bury your feelings within you, you become a graveyard. I know I was doing that as a physician when I couldn't deal with what I saw people going through.

So bring forth your feelings. Live each day allowing them to surface and guide you.

Soulution of the Day

Feel your feelings. What you bring forth will save you.

MOTHER'S DAY

Motherhood: all love begins and ends there.

— ROBERT BROWNING

What gift will you give your mother this Mother's Day?
Is a card clever enough?
Will jewels sparkle enough?
What words say enough?
There is perhaps one gift that is enough,
Your life....
Thank her for it
And live your life with the love she bestowed on you,
Then share that love with all.

Soulution of the Day

The gift of life is a mother's greatest gift.
Appreciate, respect, and acknowledge this.

AN IMPORTANT SIGN

There are many fine things which you mean to do some day, under what you think will be more favorable circumstances. But the only time that is yours is the present.

— **GRENVILLE KLEISER**

I FREQUENTLY PARTICIPATE in conferences where the organizers are quite compulsive and very concerned about keeping each speaker on schedule. So they hold up signs to keep you on target and forewarn you. When it is time to conclude your presentation, they hold up a sign that says TIME.

The organizers happily consented to my taking one of those signs, which I now use when lecturing. I hold it up in front of the audience and say, "If you take any concepts home with you from my talk, make this one of them. We are all here for a limited period of time." I want them to accept the fact that we are all mortal and shouldn't postpone living.

As long as we are in our bodies, time is an important factor. Because our bodies age and are vulnerable, our lifetime is limited and therefore extremely precious. So do what needs to be done to keep your life's presentation on schedule.

Soulution of the Day

Don't wait until your time is almost up to call home and say, "I love you." Don't bring flowers to the grave; rather, bring them home or send them to the person who is precious to you today.

RED SQUIRREL

Study nature as the countenance of God.

— KINGSLEY

A WORK OF ART crossed my path today, a red squirrel. A better artist than Picasso created him. This creature opened my heart. He connected me with something I long for — perfection in form, movement, and life. I look for him everywhere in the hopes we will meet again. I want to feed him and sustain his beauty. The world needs its red squirrels.

Soulution of the Day

You too are a work of art.
Today notice all the works of the Great Artist.

POETIC RELIEF

Poetry is language at its most distilled and most powerful.

— RITA DOVE

IF YOU DON'T WRITE POETRY, you are missing a great opportunity. The other day I greeted my wife at the door and then put away several bags of groceries. I patted myself on the back for being such a good guy and waited for her to return to the kitchen. When she did, she said, "You don't put tomatoes in the refrigerator." No "thank you," just criticism. What was my response? To write a poem entitled "Divorce."

In it I listed all my deficits, like putting tomatoes in the refrigerator, eating and walking too fast, and snoring. I read the poem to my wife, and she laughed. I love her when she laughs, so we fired the divorce lawyer, took the tomatoes out of the refrigerator, and decided to give love a chance. Now you know why I love and recommend writing poetry.

Soulution of the Day

The day you start writing, your world will change.

INSPIRATION

*Inspiration comes from the
Heart of Heaven to give the lift of wings,
and the breath of divine music
to those of us who are earthbound.*

— MARGARET SANGSTER

WHEN I SPEAK TO RESPIRATORY THERAPISTS the words *inspiration* and *inspire* relate to the act of breathing, mechanical movements of the chest and diaphragm which pull air into our lungs. Yet these words carry a much more significant meaning as well.

In many languages the word for *breath* or *inspiration* relates to our spirit and spark of life. I do not think it is an accident that this meaning is shared. After all, God breathed life into Adam through his nostrils. That first inspiration brought life into a piece of clay. Dust became alive.

We are all dust and clay until we find inspiration in our lives. When we are inspired, we change the world, not by changing others, but by changing ourselves. If everyone on this planet felt inspired and breathed life into each other, we would have a world of companionship and love.

Soulution of the Day

Inspire deeply for yourself and all those in your life.

ENJOY YOURSELF

Enjoy yourself. It's later than you think.

— CHINESE PROVERB

A PHYSICIAN, while making rounds, noticed that a patient in the hospital had the same last name as he did. Even though it was not his patient, he went into her room to talk to her. He learned she had just given birth to a stillborn child. So he spent some time helping her with grief.

Years later, he received a card from her thanking him for taking the time to be with her during that difficult period in her life. She went on to say how tired he looked, and that she had learned from the nurses how much extra time he put in caring for his patients. The card also said, "While I was in China I visited a garden and there was a plaque on the wall. I asked them to translate it for me. Roughly it said, 'Enjoy yourself. It is later than you think.' So doctor, when I read that, I thought of you and all the time you devote to your patients. Perhaps this saying is something you might ponder?"

The doctor couldn't sleep all that night and went to his office the next day and told his boss he was taking three months off. He convinced a close friend to go with him on a trip he had always wanted to take but never had the time for.

Months later when he returned to his office, he noticed that most of his patients hadn't even realized that he'd been away. It was a humbling experience. He realized he did not have to sacrifice his own needs and desires to be a good doctor. Also, since their return, his traveling companion had been diagnosed with cancer. His friend couldn't thank him enough for inviting him along and for the joyful time they had spent together.

Soulution of the Day

Sometimes it is hard to keep the balance between enjoyment and what we think we have to do. When you find you are ignoring what brings you joy, reassess the choices you are making and what priorities are running your life.

BIRD IN A CAGE

*The last of the human freedoms
is to choose one's attitudes.*

— VICTOR FRANKL

YOU'VE HEARD THE QUESTION, "Why does the caged bird sing?"
We are all birds in cages in one way or another, but we have a
choice in how we respond. I prefer to sing. It is like a prayer for me.
It calms me and makes the moment tolerable.

A friend of mine wears a cap with a picture of Tweety on it. Her
disease makes her feel like a bird in a cage, trapped in a sick body.
The hat reminds her that caged birds can still be happy and sing.
When you sing you bring harmony back into your life.

You have a choice about the quality of the sounds you make. I
know birds that give out piercing sounds to get attention when they
are lonely. I prefer to sing, dance, and laugh, but at times I do
shriek. (Of course, the way I sing gets attention, but people prefer
that I be happy and quiet for their peace and comfort!)

Soulution of the Day

*How do you respond to your cage,
and what song do you choose to sing?*

PRESCRIPTION #147

CREATING RELATIONSHIPS

*You don't develop courage by being happy
in your relationships everyday.
You develop it by surviving difficult
times and challenging adversity.*

— BARBARA DE ANGELIS

ONE EVENING, after I had given an inspiring talk, several women crowded around to ask me questions. Those who could not get close enough to me turned toward my wife and one asked, "What's it like to be married to a man like that?" She answered, loud enough for everyone to hear, "A long, hard struggle." The women looked at me in surprise only to find I was nodding my head in agreement.

My wife and Joseph Campbell agree. He wrote that marriage was an ordeal. What are the two of them trying to tell us? They are reminding us that relationships are not about individual desires and satisfactions but about creating and sharing a third entity, the relationship. Building a relationship takes work. It is an ordeal and a struggle because two people are giving birth to this new entity, and labor pains hurt.

We would see far fewer divorces if the couples involved focused on creating a marriage rather than just getting their needs met. I do not mean that one shouldn't speak up and express feelings, or that one should become a doormat. I bellow regularly, but I also say I am sorry when I know I have acted in a way that hurts my loved ones. Even our children have learned to say, "Dad, you're not in the operating room now."

I am talking about becoming a unique part of a loving relationship, a part of a team that works together to create harmony.

Soulution of the Day

*Build your relationships out of love
and hold them together with a sense of humor.*

PRESCRIPTION #148

WRESTLE WITH GOD

Your name shall no more be called Jacob,
but Israel, for you have striven with God
and with men, and have prevailed.

— GENESIS 32:28

WE ALL MUST WRESTLE with the experiences of life. Just as Jacob was left with a limp when his thigh was put out of joint, so too can our lives become disjointed when we face disasters and life-threatening illnesses. As I write this, I am listening to the news of yet another disaster. We all are wounded by tragic events, as well as by personal ones.

Like Jacob, we must all have the courage to wrestle with life. The name *Israel* means "God wrestler." Who alive isn't a God wrestler, with parts of their lives out of joint? We need to learn from Jacob and demand a blessing from every affliction.

But we first must have the courage, desire, and determination for the wrestling match. Where no will to live exists, or where there is no desire to fight for one's life, the end will be very different from Jacob's experience. Stand up and fight. That is what life is about: not to fight with and wound others, but to fight to do good, to love and survive, despite the wounds inflicted on us.

Soulution of the Day

Use each day's problems as an opportunity to learn and
prepare yourself for the day you will be called on to wrestle with God.

STIR THE POT

*The difference between stumbling blocks
and stepping stones is the way one uses them.*

— ANONYMOUS

WHEN YOU EXPERIENCE uncomfortable feelings such as gnawing unrest, sadness, irritation, or depression, do not label them as bad feelings. Your feelings are signs that something is stirring inside of you and seeking a response.

Our feelings aid and protect us. They help us to know what is going on inside of us and warn us to respond when there is danger. They are our directors and teachers.

Feelings that bubble to the surface have a purpose. When you remove your judgment of them and follow their direction, they will reveal the underlying issue so that it can be resolved.

Soulution of the Day

*When you stop resisting your feelings, you will see that they offer you a
source of wisdom and an opportunity for nourishment and growth.*

DISCIPLES

*Disciple to a philosophy, disciple to a set of
principles, disciple to a set of values,
disciple to an overriding purpose, to a
superordinate goal or a person who
represents that goal.... You are a disciple,
a follower, of your own deep values
and their source.*

— ANONYMOUS

JESUS ASKED HIS DISCIPLES to give up everything and follow him.
I do not think that today we need physically to follow someone to
attain spiritual knowledge, because the words and teachings are
available to us all.

I asked my friend Gloria a question about disciples. She writes
Heaven Letters, which come from the words she hears from God.
Here are some words she shared in answer to my question: "We are
entwined partners. Be a disciple to your own heart. Be a disciple to
truth. Your willingness to be with Me is your discipleship. Know
our oneness." I agree and feel we commence to be disciples when
we listen to the truth and to our hearts and become one.

Soulution of the Day

Become a disciple of the teachings of your heart.

WHOLENESS

*Wholeness is not about your
anatomical body but your spiritual life.*

— CARMINE BIRSAMMATO

WHAT MAKES YOU FEEL WHOLE? Certainly it is not the parts of
your body. I have met people born with no arms or who have lost
body parts because of accidents or diseases, and yet they seemed
more whole than others I know with all their parts present and
functioning.

A friend with athetoid cerebral palsy has the courage to type her
life story with her nose. She is tied into a chair so she will be able to
sit, and gagged so as not to drool on the typewriter. She is whole
and complete in her own way.

Whole human beings are immediately recognizable by their
integrity, self-awareness, and esteem. They do not need you to
make them whole. Their wholeness comes from their ability to be
creative and to call on their internal independence.

All of us must rely on others, but how many of us feel whole
only in the presence of others?

Soulution of the Day

*Decide what you need to feel whole.
Then begin to fill in the holes.*

QUESTION

We all need to find our Calcutta.

— MOTHER TERESA

I BREAK THE WORD *question* into multiple words, because these words reflect what my questions are about. Who am I? Where am I going? What should I be doing? They speak to me of my life and future — what *quest* am *I on?* They speak to me of having a calling.

The word *calling* speaks to me of a voice calling out to help guide me through the troubled waters of life. The words *voice* and *vocation* speak to me of the same search. Hopefully I will hear my true calling and not be misled or distracted.

Soulution of the Day

Keep listening for the voice.
Guides surround you and are speaking to you.
When you hear a voice, do not be afraid to question it
to be sure it is guiding you on your true quest.

KNOWLEDGE

The reason a lot of people do not recognize opportunity is because it usually goes around wearing overalls and looking like hard work.

— THOMAS EDISON

A GREAT DEAL OF KNOWLEDGE is available to all of us. With the advent of the computer, one can access knowledge of all sorts without leaving home. Does that change anything for us as individuals? Some say yes and some no.

What I see is the need for more than knowledge and access to it. We need desire, intention, determination, and the energy to do what is needed. Whether one is confronting a disease, looking for a job, or learning to play the piano, success depends on those elements. No one else can "turn on" the needed elements. Others can give you the knowledge and outline the skills necessary, but you have to put on the overalls.

In any field knowledge is important. But how the knowledge is used and how persistent one is in moving toward a goal goes way beyond what knowledge alone can do. You may have to pass a test to show you are capable, but after the test it is what you do with your knowledge that really counts.

Soulution of the Day

Mix knowledge, determination, desire, intention, and energy and come up with a nourishing life force.

PILGRIMAGE AND MARATHONS

Life is a journey, and where your finish line is has yet to be determined.

— ANONYMOUS

WE ARE ALL ON A PILGRIMAGE to a final destination. What that is for each of us, we play a large part in determining. Your choice of direction will lead you further or closer to home. Your pilgrimage is also like a marathon, in the sense of it being a long and difficult journey unless you have been trained for it.

Every day is an opportunity to train. Take a few steps, jog a short distance, and each day go a little further. Let those around you know what you are doing so they can replenish your fluids at water stops or provide nourishment.

Listen to the still, small voice as you go forward and follow the words that will direct you on your pilgrimage. To find the truth and to find yourself are really what the journey is about. I have found that I can learn a great deal running in place too, if I but listen to the inner voice. The marathon may be twenty-six miles long; the pilgrimage, however, is not about how far you go but how deeply you go into yourself.

Soulution of the Day

Train yourself daily.
Study the pilgrimages of others who have reached their destination,
and when you are ready begin yours.

RING TRUE

*You can tell the man who rings true
from the man who rings false, not by his
deeds alone, but also his desires.*

— DEMOCRITUS

WE HAVE A PRAYER BOWL at home that gives off beautiful tones when it is rubbed or struck. I wish that we as people could ring true like that bowl. When we are struck by one of life's happenings do we ring true? Do we live up to the sermons we deliver?

I always know when something doesn't ring true. Like the feeling I have when I discover that a marriage counselor has been divorced five times or when I see a fitness consultant taking a cigarette break. I want the people I deal with to live their message. I am not criticizing, I just want honesty. I demand it of myself and expect it of others.

The next time something or someone doesn't feel quite right to you, listen for the sound of the ring. Is it true?

Soulution of the Day

*Check to see if your actions ring true.
I ask myself, "What would I do now?" Ask yourself the same question!*

OCEAN

*In all things in nature
there is something of the marvelous.*

— **ARISTOTLE**

I HAVE ALWAYS BEEN attracted to the ocean. We have a vacation house on Cape Cod, and if I didn't have so many family connections here, I'd probably be living in Hawaii now. I feel close to the essence of life and creation when I stand, listen to, and watch the eternal coming and going of the waves.

In the evening the sound of the roaring surf sedates me. I have watched the ocean wash away large pieces of the land and can appreciate its force. On a deserted beach in Molokai, the Hawaiian island where a leper colony once existed, I had to rescue my wife when a large wave unexpectedly knocked her over and pulled her into the ocean.

The ocean, the mountains, and the rainbows that one sees in Hawaii remind me of the pact God made with Noah. The rainbow was the sign meant to remind us of God's pledge to not send another flood.

Soulution of the Day

Stand, watch, and listen to the rhythm of life the ocean displays.

PRESCRIPTION #157

BE A COACH

*Great opportunities to help others
seldom come, but small ones
surround us daily.*

— SALLY KOCH

WE ALL NEED COACHES, someone to point out our errors in technique, improve our skills, and not take credit when we do something well. A good coach brings out the talent in others and doesn't take all the glory for what the team does.

Think of yourself as a coach and help your friends, family, and all God's creatures to bring out their latent talents and develop their skills. People just need the right nourishment to grow; the potential is already within them. You can help it to grow. Support others when they need it and watch what you produce: a winner!

Soulution of the Day

Notice who could use a coach today, then step up to the plate.

IF ONLY

Regrets and recriminations
only hurt your soul.

— ARMAND HAMMER

HOW MANY OF US waste our precious time living in the "if onlys"? It doesn't matter what the circumstance, we can always find an if only. For instance, when a family member dies we might think: if only I had visited more often, written the letter, or said what I wanted to say before they died. Or when the stock market goes up or down, we reflect, if only I had bought or sold as I had thought I should. There are many other if onlys: if only I had asked her out, taken the job, moved to Alaska, bought the house, or said "I love you."

Regrets and if onlys are very personal. We all have moments that keep resurfacing. I could sit around and remember every patient of mine who had a problem that I couldn't diagnose until they were quite ill and say, "If only I were a better surgeon." Yet what good would it do to relive these regrets?

If your regrets and recriminations just cause you continual grief, then they are of no value and will destroy you. However, you can become a better person by assessing your if onlys. If you realize you did the best you could at the moment and forgive yourself, then they can pay countless dividends in the future.

Soulution of the Day

Discard past regrets, cleanse your conscience,
and create a new and better person.

ON THE EDGE

"Come to the edge," he said.
They said, "We are afraid."
"Come to the edge," he said. They came.
He pushed them... and they flew.

— GUILLAUME APOLLINAIRE

HAVE YOU HEARD THIS OLD ADAGE about being afraid to come to the edge of a cliff because you might fall, then when you are pushed, you fly? Well, you can do the same thing when you are out on a limb...fly.

If you have a fear of heights or flying, you may never get anywhere. It's not so hard to learn to fly. Even if you come down with a crash, at least you took a chance and felt the thrill of flying. So give it a try!

I am not talking about risking your life or possessions. I'm talking about not living in fear and allowing yourself to explore your limits. If you want to hide in the bottom of the nest all your life, that's fine, but you will not be truly living until you take the risk, come to the edge, trust, and leap into life.

Soulution of the Day

The next time you feel you are on the edge,
remember that fear keeps you stuck; action will help you to fly.

GROW DOWN

Hurry the baby as fast as you can,
Hurry him, worry him, make him a man.

— NIXON WATERMAN

THE UNWISE ARE ALL IN A HURRY to grow up and have their off-spring do the same: go to school, choose a career, get serious, and raise a family. I say "growing down" makes more sense. There are some wonderful poems about living life backward.

Just think about growing younger and looking forward to partying and being a child instead of looking ahead to more responsibilities. Dying first would be a benefit too; then you wouldn't have to worry about it anymore.

Growing down offers us a chance to face enjoyable challenges like learning to skate or ride a bike. So start reversing your life now. You will get younger each year.

Soulution of the Day

What would you do first if you knew
you were about to start growing younger?

THE INCREDIBLE EARTHWORM

All things bright and beautiful,
all creatures great and small,
all things wise and wonderful:
The Lord God made them all.

— CECIL FRANCES ALEXANDER

THE EARTHWORM is one of God's favorite creatures. It is an incredible creation because to the earthworm everything is edible. If we as elevated spiritual beings, made in the likeness of God, ate what the earthworm ate, we would die of food poisoning. That, however, is not what most impresses me and delights God. The earthworm eats all these poisons, digests them, and then eliminates a nontoxic waste material that serves as fertilizer. The earthworm will save our planet for us if we don't overwhelm it or destroy it with our lack of concern for the environment.

The earthworm spends its life caretaking, while some of us can't even throw our garbage into the proper receptacle. If the earthworm could eat glass, plastic, and metal I wouldn't be so upset, but there is a limit to its abilities. I think it is time we stopped talking about our spirits, souls, or the afterlife and get to work with the earthworm as our role model. If I ever start a business or become part of a team, I will be sure we use the earthworm as our mascot. Our motto: We can swallow anything you throw at us, turn it into fertilizer, and make it a growth experience.

Soulution of the Day

All of God's creatures are important to the plan;
we must all be good earth stewards.

THE BREAKS

When you are inspired by some great purpose, some extraordinary project, all your thoughts break their bounds: Your mind transcends limitations, your consciousness expands in every direction, and you find yourself in a new, great, and wonderful world. Dormant forces, faculties, and talents become alive, and you discover yourself to be a greater person by far than you ever dreamed yourself to be.

— PATANJALI

MY FIRST THOUGHT when I hear "break it up" is of a fight. *Breakup* reminds me of the end of a relationship, and *breakdown* makes me think of someone falling apart under stressful conditions. A break-in usually refers to illegal activities. Most "breaks" are not something we want. Even when we say "give me a break," what are we looking for? We want people to leave us alone and stop the pressure.

The break I like to hear about is not the lucky break you get that comes along by chance, but the *breakthrough*. This word gives me a feeling that something has happened that enlightens and alters you in a way that will improve your life and that of others.

Please keep working to break through into a life of love and healing. All the breakthroughs the great prophets had can be used to benefit our lives and help bring meaning. So take your old life and break it up. Don't live waiting for the lucky break. Break up with the people in your past who led you astray, and don't be afraid of a breakdown either. You will come out of the darkness and break through into the light.

Soulution of the Day

You deserve a break today…a breakthrough.

FATHER'S DAY

*You are the bows from which your children
as living arrows are sent forth.*

— KAHLIL GIBRAN

IT IS MY BELIEF that on Father's Day I should bestow gifts on all my children. They should not be required to give me anything, because it was their mother and I who created them. They were not asked whether they wished to be created and born into this life.

The greatest gift I can give them is my love. I have learned with the years how to be better at loving than I was when they were young. I have apologized for my inadequacies and ask them to teach me to be a better father. They are very tolerant and very good teachers.

One son regularly called home to leave very critical messages on the answering machine when he was a teenager. He and I now work together as a team to help other wounded souls. I told him the other day I still had the tapes. He said, "I think you can discard them now."

I answered, "No, you may have a son, and someday he'll call and leave a message that will break your heart. Then I will play your tapes to remind you that with love, you and your child can heal your relationship too."

Soulution of the Day

*If you are a father, don't ask for love on Father's Day
but bestow it on those who gave you the gift of fatherhood.*

PRESCRIPTION #**164**

LOUIE, LOUIE

*It is during our darkest moments
that we must focus to see the light.*

— TAYLOR BENSON

I ATTENDED COLGATE UNIVERSITY in Hamilton, New York.
Hamilton is a tiny town with only one little, old movie theater. The
projectionist was named Louie. He didn't pay much attention to
what he was doing and often showed the reels in the wrong order.
Occasionally he would doze off. The film on the screen would go
out of focus and all the people in the theater would yell, "Focus,
Louie, focus." That always got an immediate result.

Much of our lives are wasted because we focus too much on
meaningless things, worries, and nonsense. So sit down and ask
yourself what you want to focus on and what is important to you. I
am not talking about what material things you want to accumulate,
I am talking about your life. Focus, Louie, focus…on life, relationships, work, and family. Keep your main feature in focus on the big
screen of life.

Soulution of the Day

*Don't doze off in the middle of your life:
keep focused on what is truly important.*

WRINKLES

If wrinkles must be written upon our brows,
let them not be written upon the heart.
The spirit should never grow old.

— JOHN KENNETH GALBRAITH

WHEN YOU WASH SOMETHING, it can come out wrinkled. That's life! Just remember, if God puts you through the wringer it's because you're worth laundering. If I were given the choice between dying young and developing wrinkles, the answer would be clear to me. I choose life, come what may, regardless of old age and wrinkles.

When we as a society respect wrinkles rather than spending time and money trying to remove or hide them, we will all have taken a step forward. In countries where people regularly live to be one hundred, people lie about their age. They tell you they are older than they are. Why? Because those with wrinkles are respected. The day we revere wrinkles and the wisdom that goes with them will be a turning point toward a healthier and happier society.

Soulution of the Day

Next time you look in the mirror count your wrinkles and feel proud.

A DAY OF REST

*The Sabbath is God's special present to the
working man, and one of its chief objects is
to prolong his life, and preserve efficient his
working tone. The savings bank of human
existence is the weekly Sabbath.*

— WILLIAM G. BLAIKIE

I HAVE ALWAYS FELT THAT GOD wanted us to be aware of our
mortality so that we would use our time wisely. It occurs to me that
the Sabbath speaks of the same thing. God rested on the seventh
day, and we should see it as a holy day and do the same thing. We
are asked to celebrate the day and time and use it in a different way.

It is hard for me to believe that the Creator really needed a rest
with His unlimited resources. I think the rest day was created to
make us think about what we are doing with our lives. According
to some religions, if we are working on the Sabbath we are sinning
and wasting our time. But if we are contributing to life and
creation, then the day is being used properly. I don't think one
literally has to sit and do nothing, but we must not be working.

So use the seventh day to create and be aware of your time, just
as God wants you to be.

Soulution of the Day

*Pick a day to be your Sabbath each week.
We all have work to do, but on the seventh day put your work aside
and take the day to rest and re-create.*

GUARANTEED HAPPINESS

Giving is a miracle that can transform the heaviest hearts.

— KENT NERBURN, *SIMPLE TRUTHS*

WHAT DO YOU THINK can guarantee happiness? A poem I read entitled "How to Be Happy" revealed a simple answer. It said, "Do something for somebody, quick!"

Now, you may think you have more problems than anyone else on the planet, so perhaps this answer seems like it wouldn't work for you. But if you first accept the fact that you are not the only one with problems, and then follow what the poem states, you will be surprised at the outcome. So "even if your earthly affairs are in a terrible whirl, do something for somebody, quick!"

When I think about how I can help others I feel a lot better than I do when I am dwelling on my problems. When I follow the advice in the poem and find others to help, I have noticed how many people start doing nice things for me in return.

So do something for somebody today and watch what happens in your life. Even small gifts of love like sending a greeting card or remembering someone's birthday can reconnect us with life and its meaning.

Soulution of the Day

Do it quick!

BREEZES, RIPPLES, AND SEEDS

*We did not weave the web of life — we are
merely a strand in it. Whatever we do
to the web, we do to ourselves.*

— CHIEF SEATTLE

IT OCCURS TO ME that what we do has the same effect as a butterfly flapping its wings. Now, the small movement of butterfly wings may not seem impressive to you, but it actually alters the world's air currents and affects us all.

In the same way that dandelion seeds can move in the wind, when you plant your seeds in the earth, you are having an effect on what will grow. Even a small pebble thrown into a pond causes change. The ripples created by your actions will spread out and change the nature of all life.

Soulution of the Day

*Please remember you are the one who casts seeds, creates breezes,
and makes waves by your life, words, and actions.
So think about what you do; it affects us all and creates
a future for the world's children.*

PRESCRIPTION #169

BASEBALL

Never let the fear of striking out get in your way.

— **Babe Ruth**

THERE ARE MANY LESSONS to be learned from baseball. The first is that it isn't over until it's over. Until the last out you still have a chance. That is the way we all need to live; you don't ever give up if you want to be a winner.

You also must show up for practice. You may be fortunate to have been born with a set of genes that gives you a body with great potential, but if you don't show up for practice you are not going to make the team. Performance is what counts, not appearance. How do you get to Carnegie Hall? Practice, practice, practice.

The other lesson to remember is that you don't have to be a big leaguer to enjoy playing the game. You can learn from children about the enjoyment of playing. They do not worry about how they look or how good they are or wonder if people will laugh at them if they drop the ball and strike out. They just run, play, and have fun.

So enjoy playing and take a chance. Never give up until the game of life is over.

Soulution of the Day

Life is a baseball game.
Do you want to advance to the plate and take a swing
or sit in the dugout and watch?

BE IN THE NOW

Remember: be here now.

— RAM DASS

WHEN GOD CREATED THE UNIVERSE it was *now*. This moment we are experiencing is also now. You can't say to creation, "I'll do it later," because the universe only knows now. So whenever you get around to it, it will be now.

Time is our creation. It does not exist for the divine Creator, spirit, or energy. Time does exist for matter, but it is only measured by us. The only time we can actually experience is the now. Everything you need is found in the present, all power, love, and healing is in the *now*.

Soulution of the Day

Stay focused in the now and live in the moment;
it is really all we have.

THE EXTREMES

It is easy to sit up and take notice;
what is difficult is getting up
and taking action.

— AL BATT

NO, "THE EXTREMES" are not a singing group. They are the choices we have to make. Now, you may say you want everything in moderation and don't like to be extreme in anything you choose. But without extremes, there is no depth or challenge in your life.

What do you believe in? What are you here to do? You have to make some choices when you see life and nature being destroyed. The truth is we all have to take extreme measures at times. It is not a question of whether you will be extreme, but a question of what you will be extreme about.

What is important to you? Or is nothing important to you, so you take the extreme position of never speaking up for a worthy cause or person?

I find that extremely upsetting.

Soulution of the Day

Be willing to take a stand for something you believe in,
even if it means going to extremes.

OUT ON A LIMB

I gave my word to this tree, the forest and to all the people, that my feet would not touch the ground until I had done everything in my power to make the world aware of this problem and to stop the destruction.

— JULIA BUTTERFLY HILL,
THE LUNA TREE SIT

I DON'T MIND GOING OUT ON A LIMB when I know that what I am reaching for and risking injury for is worthwhile. I'll crawl out there so that people will stop, look, and listen. I know what I am out there for is the truth and that it needs to be acknowledged and responded to.

When you take the risk to go out on a limb for something you believe in, support will come. The limb will not break; it will bend and sway in the face of adversity until the weight is shared by others.

Don't be afraid to go out on a limb and speak your truth to the powers that be. The power of one is a great thing. Use it wisely, and you will be amazed at how many people will climb out on the limb with you and be supported.

Soulution of the Day

What are you willing to go out on a limb for?

SHAVE IT OFF

I can't shave your head;
your sons have threatened me if I do that.

— ANTHONY PETONITO

IN THE MID-1970S when men were wearing their hair down to their shoulders, I had the urge to shave my head. This urge drove me crazy, and I kept telling my wife, four sons, and daughter what I wanted to do. Their reaction ranged from "Are you nuts?" to "Don't you dare embarrass us any more than you already have!"

When I told my barber, Anthony Petonito, he shrugged and told me that my sons had already told him, "Don't you dare do it." Months went by, and then that summer I promised Anthony if he shaved my head I would leave town on vacation and no one would know. He finally did it.

I went back to the office, and my wife came in and asked for me. She saw the back of my head and didn't know it was me. When I turned, she screamed. At the hospital, people were more open with me and shared their troubles because I seemed more vulnerable.

Today the style has caught on, but not my meaning. For me, the bare head relates to my experience as an infant when my grandmother massaged my head, but even more so my spiritual journey. Monks shave their heads as a spiritual uncovering. When I read about the tonsure or uncovering, I knew I needed to do the same so that I could find and reveal my spiritual self.

Soulution of the Day

You don't have to shave your head, but you do have to
uncover your true self if you are to live your life fully.

WORD POWER

Words have no legs, yet they walk.

— MALI PROVERB

SOMETIMES WE REALLY NEED TO LISTEN to what we say. Think of all the things people say about their hearts when they are hurting: I'm downhearted, my heart is broken, the pain was heartfelt, my heart cries for you, sighs for you, and dies for you. Wow, do we ever stop and listen to what we are saying and doing to ourselves? We need to be aware when we make these statements that we are hurting ourselves and prolonging the pain we do not know how to deal with in our lives.

Words can be a trigger to let us know we need to take action. Be aware of what you say and what message your words are sending to you and others. If it is breaking your heart to remember or think about something, then get help. No, not a heart transplant, but some emotional glue. You'll find it in the medicine cabinet under love and laughter. Love is the manufacturer of your heart and guarantees it for a long lifetime if you use your heart to keep loving regularly. When cracks appear in your heart love will repair it effectively. For short-term help and to get you restarted, remember that humor and joy are wonderful cements to hold things together until the warranty kicks in and love restores you.

Soulution of the Day

When your words are turning against you remember to go to your "medicine cabinet" and look for the remedy.

GUILT

Guilt: the gift that keeps on giving.

— ERMA BOMBECK

GUILT CAN BE EITHER HEALTHY or unhealthy. It can lead to a change in your behavior or not. You can spend your life behind bars and never feel guilty about what you were convicted of, or you can use the guilt to grow. When all the Cains feel guilt over killing their brother, Abel, then we will be able to begin to heal the wounds of the planet.

There is healthy guilt that leads you to feel sorrow for your behavior and to seek to make amends for your actions. When you do, understanding, forgiveness, and healing come together and you can move on.

Those who feel no guilt are emotionally unhealthy and a danger to society and all living things. But those who feel guilty about everything and can never let it go do not contribute to the betterment of society either.

I carried a spider out of the house today because I found it impossible to kill it just for my convenience. I am proud of myself and the fact that I felt turmoil over killing another living thing. I would prefer to die free of guilt, forgiving myself and even my assassin, rather than die hating.

Soulution of the Day

Do not avoid guilt feelings; they are a sign of your mental health.
Listen to them and follow their guidance.

PROCRASTINATION

It's the start that stops most people.

— DON SHULA

OUR EXCUSES ARE ENDLESS: I'll do it tomorrow, as soon as I get the time, I have a note on my desk to remind me, and so on and so forth. There are no tomorrows, there are only todays. If you don't get started today, you may never do it.

There must be fear involved, or you would have started by now. Nothing is holding you back except you. If you are procrastinating, then ask yourself, "What am I afraid of? What is the risk involved? What do I really want to do?" Get in touch with your desires and ask yourself what is holding you back. Acknowledge these barriers and begin your task with one small step. You can set your own pace and do it your own way, so why wait?

Soulution of the Day

Stop waiting for the "right time." It is here now.

WHO DID THAT?

St. Francis was led to love all things which he knew had the same origin as he, and in which he recognized the goodness of God. For he followed his Well-Beloved everywhere and in every trace of Him to be found in His creatures, he made of all things a ladder to reach His throne.

— POPE PIUS XI,
LETTER ON SAINT FRANCIS OF ASSISI

"WHO DID THAT?" Those words tend to frighten most of us because they remind us of our parents wanting to know who did something they weren't happy about.

But what about the times when you see beauty before you? Do you stop and think, "Who did that?" The next time you see a work of art, stop and reflect on its creator.

When you see a flower, a beautiful painting, a child, or look in the mirror, stop and wonder, "Who did that?" If you are aware of the precious works of art around you, you will take better care of them and yourself. The artist went to a lot of trouble to create us all, so don't destroy the artwork. The treasures of the ages need to be preserved.

A thousand-year-old tree deserves to be looked at in awe. Each new creation, be it a tiny wildflower arising out of the earth or a baby elephant, is a work of art. Ask who the artist is and get to know the Creator better.

Soulution of the Day

*Try to see everything as a precious work of art today. Then ask yourself,
"Who did that?" The world will become your art gallery.*

LIFESAVING TIME

*Yesterday is but today's memory
and tomorrow is today's dream.*

— KAHLIL GIBRAN

I SIT AND LOOK AT A PHOTOGRAPH of one of our sons and think about how much it looks like his son, our grandchild. I hope my son is spending time with his son. Unlike me, I hope he will not look at his son's picture thirty years later and wish he could turn back the clock and spend more time together.

It is not fair that we cannot go back to earlier times after we become wise enough to know how we should have used the time. I want to go back and enjoy my children more. I want to be able to just sit with them and love them in ways I wasn't wise enough to do years ago. It is not fair that we have to learn from experience.

That is why I will send these words to you so you will not waste your life but instead set your clock to lifesaving time and let it apply all year round. Then years from now you will pick up a photograph and smile recalling wonderful moments and the good feelings you are left with rather than the desire to go back and try again to get it right.

Soulution of the Day

Never mind daylight saving time; institute lifesaving time now.

PRESCRIPTION #179

QUIET DOWN

*A happy life must be to a great extent a
quiet life, for it is only in an atmosphere of
quiet that true joy can live.*

— BERTRAND RUSSELL

WE HAVE FILLED OUR LIVES with meaningless activities and
eliminated quiet time. Some people equate being quiet with being
bored. They think if you are not doing something all the time and
going from place to place, that you will be bored. That couldn't be
farther from the truth. I read that Charles Darwin, after traveling
around the world, spent the rest of his life in his own home.

What about children who can use a little rest period or quiet
time to be creative and just play, instead of being taken to another
activity every minute they are not in school?

Some families and communities are creating "do nothing days"
so they can stay home and learn that quiet time can be a better
activity than driving everyone everywhere. The message is to slow
down and live rather than continually doing something and being
somewhere. Who cares what the neighbors think when they see
you sitting around the house?

Quiet time together as a family may include things like playing
in the yard, sharing a board game, or just taking a walk. We had
a swimming pool in the backyard of our first home so our five
children could enjoy staying home and spending time together.
The kids in the neighborhood all had a great time at the pool too.

Soulution of the Day

*You can miss a lot in your life if you do not take the time
to slow down and live.*

COMMUNICATION

*If you talk to a man in a language
he understands, that goes to his head.
If you talk to him in his language,
that goes to his heart.*

— NELSON MANDELA

YOU MAY WONDER IF PEOPLE HEAR what we are saying when they are ill or unconscious and whether or not you should try to communicate with them. I believe people hear when they are under anesthesia, in a coma, or asleep. Even infants hear while they are still in the uterus. I can assure you that the senile and individuals with Alzheimer's disease hear you too. Although they may not be able to communicate, they are still aware at some level of consciousness.

Talk to them, and let them know of your love. Care for them from your heart, because to do it out of guilt will be felt by them and also by you. Caring for someone for unhealthy reasons will take its toll on both the caregiver and the person requiring care.

There are other ways to communicate. You can talk with your touch; embrace and massage them. I often bring an infant, kitten, or puppy with me and place it in their arms. Seeing them smile and react tells me they are very much alive, even if they have a dysfunctional body or mind. Every connection has value and brings us closer to each other.

Soulution of the Day

*Even when you think someone is beyond communication,
don't give up. There is always a way to share love.*

PRESCRIPTION #181

YOUR NATURE

For in the true nature of things, if we rightly consider, every green tree is far more glorious than if it were made of gold and silver.

— MARTIN LUTHER

THE NEXT TIME your family complains about your behavior, just tell them, "That's my nature." That ought to get them off your back, and if you keep acting up long enough, they will eventually stop complaining. Of course, what they say behind your back won't be very nice!

Why are we so resistant to having a *second* nature? Why not learn from others and change our behavior? Qualities that are useful in the business world lead to a high rate of divorce and employee turnover. Why can't our nature be one of kindness and willingness to change?

Nature is kind, though it has its stormy moments and its seasons. If we imitate nature we can vary but still be our true selves rather than protecting our artificial nature with statements that are excuses, explain nothing, and display our rigidity and unwillingness to come out from behind the wall and expose our real nature.

Soulution of the Day

Let nature take its true course with you.

PRESCRIPTION #182

OLIVE OIL

*Following the course of least resistance
makes for crooked rivers and crooked men.*

— LANNY HENNINGER

OLIVE OIL is a healthy fat and should be used to cook foods, poured over salads, and added to your recipes. In countries where olive oil is a standard part of the diet, the results are apparent in how heart healthy the people are. However, being heart healthy comes from more than just ingesting olive oil, but the oil is a good teacher.

The oil is created by crushing the beautiful olives that are picked to make the oil. We are all under pressure most of the time owing to our lifestyles. Often we become bitter, restless, resentful, and more. However, the olive knows that the pressures of life make us what we are and can be used to create something better. Perhaps if we too understood this, we would suffer less the "slings and arrows of outrageous fortune."

Do not be afraid of the pressure. Use it to guide you just as it birthed you, and use its energy to push you forward into a meaningful life.

Soulution of the Day

*The easy way out will lead you to places you don't want to go.
Sometimes a little crushing and pressure are just what you need.*

MISTAKES CAN BE GOOD TEACHERS

The only real mistake is the one from which we learn nothing.

— JOHN POWELL

WHAT IS A MISTAKE? For most of us, saying "I made a mistake" means either we did the wrong thing or we did something incorrectly. But is doing something wrong the worst outcome?

Mistakes can be our teachers. They can redefine our goals and tasks and therefore turn out to be beneficial. Often we focus on our mistakes and spend energy judging ourselves because of them. Instead, be patient and await their lessons and teachings, which are not always immediately apparent.

I have learned a lot from my mistakes and therefore no longer label them "mistakes." Sometimes the direction they have sent me in turned out better than the one I would have otherwise gone. So expect to make mistakes. Say, "I am sorry" when they affect others and then learn from them.

Soulution of the Day

Try to see your "mistakes" in a new light today.

ADDICTIONS

*People spend a lifetime searching for
happiness; looking for peace. They chase idle
dreams, addictions, religions, even other
people, hoping to fill the emptiness that
plagues them. The irony is the only place
they ever needed to search was within.*

— RAMONA L. ANDERSON

WHAT ARE WE SEARCHING for when we become addicted to drugs, alcohol, food, sex, money, aberrant behaviors, and more? What feelings are we searching for that are missing? Why do we become self-destructive and willing to give up our lives to substances and actions that separate us from what we really desire?

I don't believe it is an accident that we call alcohol "spirits" and talk about getting "high" on drugs. But you are never going to find love, spirituality, and our Creator in bottles, boxes, pills, food, or any material things.

I believe addicts are looking for love and a place of peace and oneness. So off they go, into their addiction, looking to forget their feelings of emptiness and lack of self-esteem, love, and worth. Except it doesn't work! It doesn't heal you or your life, and it separates you from the people you want to be close to.

There is only one addiction that can provide you with everything you want out of life. Become addicted to love. Go inside and open your heart to one Universal Healer: love.

Soulution of the Day

*Whether you like yourself or not, love, love, love. Overdose regularly.
Seek to get high on loving yourself and others. The only known
side effect is that love is blind to the faults of others, and that's not so bad
when you consider what other addicts are going through.*

SUMMER

*Turn your face to the sun
and the shadows fall behind you.*

— MAORI PROVERB

SUMMERTIME, and the living is easy. Why? Because when you face the light, there are no shadows to be seen. Summer also offers us the opportunity to spend time outdoors among nature's living things. When we communicate and become one with nature we find wisdom not available to us anywhere else. Nature has the answers.

So go forth in summer and feel the gift of the warm sun on your skin and observe the elements of nature interacting. Take a summer vacation or summer Sabbath time during which you can learn to be, and not just do. Find the corner of the universe that brings you peace and then carry it with you in your mind's eye when you leave. That way you can always go within and find that peace again.

When nature surrounds you, listen. Listen to its rhythm, and listen to your rhythm. They are both related to creation. Whenever you experience difficult times you can return to this moment of summer and heal yourself.

Soulution of the Day

*Let your light bring all the elements of summer to others,
no matter what season it is.*

PRESCRIPTION #186

SAND DOLLARS

*It is the greatest of all mistakes
to do nothing because you can only
do little — do what you can.*

— SYDNEY SMITH

PERHAPS YOU HAVE HEARD THE STORY about the boy on the beach throwing washed-up sand dollars back into the water.

A man walks by and asks, "Why are you doing that? There are thousands of them washed up. You can't make a difference."

The boy picks one up and throws it back into the ocean, "I did for that one."

Remember, by changing one life you change the world. Every action has its effects. So make a difference and help someone get back into the ocean of life. You need not risk your life carrying them through the surf, but find out what they need to get back into the swim. Then help them do it.

Soulution of the Day

*Make a difference; throw one sand dollar back,
and you will be doing your part.*

SUNSET

When the day ends and the sun sets,
I let my troubles go.

— **ALBERT SCHWEITZER**

JUST AS I WOULD URGE YOU to start each day as if you were the sun rising anew, I would also ask you to release all your worries and troubles when the sun sets. Let them go with the sun, or you will not be able to arise free of burdens and begin the next new day.

If you hold onto your problems through the night, you begin to lose any sense of order in your life. There is no longer any night or day, just time to remain awake, to worry and fear the coming day, and to regret the restless night.

When you watch the sunset, let your worries go with it. See them burning up in the brilliant colors. Allow the beauty to remind you there is more to life than troubles!

Soulution of the Day

When you put your troubles away with the sunset,
you make room for blessings to fill the next day.

NIGHT SKY THERAPY

The heavens declare the glory of God.

— BEN ZION

LAST NIGHT I walked out of the house with our little dog, Furphy, and looked up into the night sky. The cloudless canopy was filled with an endless display of stars and left me feeling grateful and in awe.

Who knows or cares how it all got there. The fact is we are here and a part of the awesomeness of the universe. I felt uplifted and at peace after a few moments of gazing upward at the night sky.

I think we could all save a fortune on therapists if we just went out every evening and looked up at the sky. And just think what it would be like if people in the psychiatric wards and those in prison cells viewed the night sky every evening. I think they would be changed and healed by the exposure to the unexplainable beauty.

Soulution of the Day

The next time you need therapy, try gazing at the night sky.

HAPPY AT WORK

*I was surrounded
by miserable people so I told them, "I quit."*

— HOSPITAL WARD SECRETARY

ONCE I THANKED A MEDICAL SECRETARY at the hospital for her wonderful attitude and asked her for her full name because I wanted to give her a pin with her name on it as a gift. She said, "Sit down." I did, and she went on, "When I took this job I was surrounded by miserable people — the doctors and nurses. The patients weren't a problem. I went to the office to quit, but they told me I had to give two weeks' notice. I got up miserable every day for two weeks. When it was my last day I got up happy and went to work happy. I noticed something; all the people around me were happy. So I didn't quit. I decided to come in happy instead."

The kind of choice she made can work for all of us. You are in charge of your life and your attitude. Change one or the other according to your needs and desires, and you too can be happy. If you don't want to be happy you can make that choice too. No one can force you to be happy if you would rather whine and complain.

I love what Tom Hanks said in *A League of Their Own:* "There's no crying in baseball." As you play the game of life, remember that it's your attitude and choices that determine the outcome.

Soulution of the Day

*If you are in a difficult environment or situation,
try changing the attitude you bring to it. If that doesn't work,
perhaps it is time to move on.*

YOU HAVEN'T CHANGED A BIT

It takes a lot of courage to release the familiar and seemingly secure, to embrace the new. But there is no real security in what is no longer meaningful. There is more security in the adventurous and exciting, for in movement there is life, and in change there is power.

— ALAN COHEN

YOU MEET SOMEONE you haven't seen in years and she says, "You haven't changed a bit." Is that a compliment or a criticism? It depends what she is referring to.

If you fail to encourage change and growth in your life, perhaps you are afraid and prefer to remain in risk-free situations. The date changes every day, and so should you. We all need to keep growing to make our lives meaningful and to stimulate our bodies with the will to live.

Someone who is living an unchanged life is not communicating a will to live but a boredom that will lead to illness. But those who remain open to new ideas and experiences are sending "live messages" to their body and spirit.

All athletes know you need to be flexible to not injure yourself. So stretch your limits and reach out for what you were once afraid to attempt. Enlarge yourself and change your goals so that when you return for your fiftieth reunion, no one will tell you that you haven't changed a bit.

Soulution of the Day

Take a risk and step out of your familiar routine today.

SACRIFICE

Let me be born again and again on the wheel of rebirth so again and again I may offer this body for the benefit of others.

— HINDU MYTH

WHAT IS THE RESULT of your stepping into the holy fire? What can you burn off that will give you life? When you destroy yourself in holy fire you do not sacrifice anything. To sacrifice is to give up something and to go on living. When you truly serve others you are sacrificing but at the same time creating a life that cannot be destroyed.

Sacrifice, as I see it, can be the giving up of something to achieve a greater goal. The holy fire burns away the meaningless and leaves the essence. When the smoke and soot cleanse us, we are left with a golden vessel ready to carry the essence of life.

Do not be afraid to step forth and sacrifice willingly to attain greater things. Do not fear the fire, because it will not burn you. It will energize you and clear the way for you just as a forest fire prepares the soil for new growth. Move on and give up what weighs you down and slows your passage. What you sacrifice will nourish others and heal you.

Soulution of the Day

There is no sacrifice when it is done for love.

CHERISHED CREATIONS

God loves you just the way you are.

— INSCRIPTION ON A CUP
IN THE SIEGEL HOUSEHOLD

ONE MORNING I came into the kitchen to find my wife had lined up several cups with missing handles. She explained that I had jammed them into the dishwasher with disastrous results. "Please dispose of them in the recycling bin," she ordered.

"No, dear, I can drink from a cup with no handle," I replied.

Her look told me that I should either dispose of them or hire a marriage counselor. So I packed them up and took them to our vacation house and hid them in the kitchen cabinet. A few weeks later we went on vacation. I knew when she opened the cabinet that I would be in big trouble. So I ran away from home, that is, went for a run.

Why do I believe in a higher power? Because after running on the same road for twenty years and never finding anything, that morning lying in the middle of the road was a cup with a broken handle. I knew God had left it for me, so I ran over and picked it up. On it were pictured two chubby elephants embracing and the words, "God loves you just the way you are." I brought it home and showed it to my wife. Now that cup and all the other cups are an accepted part of our family again, and so am I!

Soulution of the Day

*You are perfect and loved. God cherishes you just the way you are,
even if you have a broken handle.*

GOOD FRIENDS

Friendship improves happiness and abates misery, by the doubling of our joy and the dividing of our grief.

— CICERO

WHAT IS A FRIEND? To me it is someone who knows your faults and still sees the divine in you. A friend will love you despite your imperfections. A friend is someone who is there for you when you have the courage to ask for help. A friend is also someone who can say no to you and still remain a friend.

A friend points out your imperfections, not to blame you for them but to help you become better at what you are doing, just as a coach would talk to an athlete. A friend always answers your calls even when you are driving them crazy.

A friend never talks about who is right but rather listens to how you are feeling. A friend will not judge without taking the time to understand and can forgive, let go of the past, and continue to love. Probably the most important thing a friend does is never to abandon you, no matter what you do.

Soulution of the Day

Do something to acknowledge a good friend today and remember to be one as well.

PRESCRIPTION #194

FEAR LESS

*All healing is essentially
the release from fear.*

— A COURSE IN MIRACLES

THE NEXT TIME you dream of a monster chasing you, turn, confront the monster, and watch what happens. Once you have dealt with the fear the dream will stop. The same is true in our lives; we must face our fears in order to heal them.

Our brain is wired so that fear can protect us from life-threatening situations and help us to react quickly. If you see a rattlesnake before you, your brain will bypass conscious evaluation of the danger and make you freeze so that the snake is not attracted by your motion.

But what happens if you think every stick is a poisonous snake? You are going to get nowhere. Abnormal fear can paralyze us. We must face our monsters and work out things that can be done to help us through the fear.

Music can soothe, heal, and relax us. Visualization and meditation can help reprogram the system. Physical activity produces natural antidepressants, that can help us feel better. Create a program that works for you and will help resolve your fear and tension.

Soulution of the Day

*The following quote by Dr. Robert Anthony offers good advice
for tackling your fears: "Overcoming fear and worry
can be accomplished by living a day at a time or even a moment at a time.
Your worries will be cut down to nothing."*

PRESCRIPTION #195

SELL IT

*Herman Grimhoffer was stuck in an elevator
for four hours. Upon his release he had sold
the elevator operator a new Cadillac.*

— MATTY SIMMONS

WHEN I FIRST BEGAN TO SPEAK about my experience with cancer patients, I encountered anger and opposition from the medical profession. When I was interviewed on all the well-known talk shows, I was constantly being challenged for my beliefs. Trying to sell my ideas made me an object of everyone's anger. My beliefs did not fit the establishment's beliefs.

I learned to tell stories so that my ideas would not confront others' belief systems too intensely. I also learned to listen to others' anecdotes and stories as they told about their ideas and experiences. I learned to ask and not tell. I found the best way to sell my ideas was to let another person share his experience of my techniques and how they worked for him.

When I told other doctors how to help patients, I encountered a lot of disagreement. But when I asked them if they wanted to help patients, the answer was always yes. It is much easier to sell new ideas when you are both in agreement on the basic premise.

I am not trying to sell material things, but I am trying to sell humanistic medical care. I still have my moments when I forget to share my ideas in a nonconfronting way. I still have some work to do in getting all medical professionals to stop dealing with patients and start caring for them.

Soulution of the Day

*If your goals are admirable and beneficial,
then learn how to sell them to others and become a traveling salesman.*

ORDER

We must learn to let go, to give up,
to make room for the things
we have prayed for and desired.

— CHARLES FILLMORE

EVERY DAY I AM OUT OF CONTROL. No, I do not mean I have no control over my behavior, but I do mean I am not in control of the events that present themselves to me, my family, and my life. What can I control? Only my thoughts and my response to events beyond my control.

I have learned to create order amid the uncontrollable chaos called life. By becoming one with life and the process of living, I can stop judging, fighting, and struggling with what is. I can stop denying and wishing and start living.

Let go of the need to control, and put everything in the hands of a higher authority. It will restore order and peace of mind. When you do, you will ultimately control your life and find peace on earth. You cannot change other people, and you cannot alter the past. All you can do is surrender to divine order.

Soulution of the Day

Restore order in your life by letting go of the need to control.

DANGER

*Never in all history has mankind
faced such a monstrous danger.*

— HARRY EMERSON FOSDICK

SINCE THE CREATION OF ATOMIC WEAPONS, we have continually felt we are in the most dangerous period in the history of our planet. If we use fear intelligently, we will resolve the problem. Just as fear of diseases and earthquakes has led us to take preventive measures, we can do the same with the dangers of war. We must be motivated by the fear to remove the threat rather than just reacting to it and wrapping our homes in plastic.

We cannot avoid life. We must live now and not misuse the gifts of power and technology but rather use them to improve life so there is nothing to kill or die for.

Politicians of the past sound psychotic when you read their quotes about the benefits of war. People die when countries go to war. As a comedian said, "We need war to teach geography." Other than that there is no advantage.

Soulution of the Day

Use your fears to motivate you to make the needed changes.

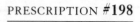

PRESCRIPTION #198

PASSAGES

*So often we look at a calendar of days
as merely a symbol of the passage of time.
We forget why we are on this earth.
We forget that there is a reason for all of the
pain and all of the struggles. We forget that
we were put on earth to learn something.*

— LYNN V. ANDREWS

LIFE IS A SERIES OF PASSAGES. Some are noted and celebrated with rituals that lead us to stop and recognize these significant rites of passage. By paying attention to these special times of change and initiation, we become more aware of our place in life.

The passage into adulthood is particularly significant. One cannot remain a child forever. There are responsibilities that we need to face and confront if we are to become whole human beings. To refuse the rites of passage may remove you from all responsibility, but it will also deny you a full life.

Life moves on and is never stagnant. You cannot stop life. It is like a river whose waters cannot be entered in the same place from moment to moment. We must learn to go with the flow and not allow our resistance to dam up our life.

Soulution of the Day

*Appreciate the journey, the passages, the twists and the turns;
they are all the stages of your life.*

DEAR GOD

Faith is the highest passion in a human being. Many in every generation may not come that far, but none comes further.

— SØREN KIERKEGAARD

"**DEAR GOD, I AM MAD AS HELL,** or heaven, at you. I am sick and tired of being sick and tired. You either make me well or let me die. You have done a lousy job, and that's putting it mildly, with this world. What about all the wars and suffering of innocent people. What sense does it make? Why did you do this?

"If you are responsible and all-powerful, why not fix things, and if you are not responsible and all-powerful, then say so and let us move on. To let things go on this way makes no sense. So get me out of here or fix things tonight."

I know a woman who went to bed after screaming those words to God. What do you think happened? Nothing? You're wrong. She woke up cured of her disease. Was it you, God? Who knows? But what I do know is when you have the passion she had or total faith and belief in God, and give your troubles to him or her, things do change.

Soulution of the Day

Passion or faith? Choose your path to healing.

CHOCOLATE

*Strength is the capacity to break a chocolate
bar into four pieces with your bare hands —
and then eat just one of the pieces.*

— JUDITH VIORST

CHOCOLATE AFFECTS US because of its chemical nature. It is even good for us because it contains antioxidants. It makes us feel good, and it also tastes good and is a treat to enjoy. Some people say eating chocolate simulates the feeling of being in love.

Sometimes we are so busy denying our needs that chocolate becomes an addiction. It is always available, and we think we deserve a treat because our life seems difficult and unfair. It can be unhealthy to consume quarts of chocolate ice cream or even low-fat chocolate frozen yogurt. But you say, "So what! Look at what I am going through, so why deny myself chocolate?"

There comes a point when what is good for you can become self-destructive. I do not want to die without experiencing the taste of chocolate, but I do not want chocolate to be what kills me. I can see having a dish of chocolate ice cream as a gift to myself, and I can see saying no to a second dish of chocolate ice cream as a gift to myself.

What we need to do is find a life that provides us with the chemistry of chocolate within our bodies. When we do, addictions and excessive needs will cease. Instead of substituting an artificial simulation for love, we need to find the real thing.

Soulution of the Day

All I really need is love, but a little chocolate now and then doesn't hurt!

(Lucy, Peanuts)

WHAT IF?

Of course you can't unfry an egg, but there is no law against thinking about it.

— DON HEROLD

IF YOU HAD YOUR LIFE TO LIVE OVER, what would you do differently? Poems and stories reflecting on the past talk about wishing you had picked daisies, eaten more ice cream, taken fewer things seriously, been sillier, wore only purple, and paid less attention to what others thought and being perfect.

Maybe we should take a lesson from the angels. We are told that angels can fly because they take themselves lightly — they are not constantly involved in the opinions of others and the seriousness of every situation. Will Durant said, "Gaiety is wiser than wisdom."

The wise know what can go wrong tomorrow and confront the day seriously. The lighthearted can still enjoy today, even though they know the seriousness of tomorrow. Which day would you prefer? As Don Herold shares, "If nations declared international carnivals instead of international wars, how much better that would be!"

So just ask yourself, "If I had the last several years of my life to live over again, what would I do differently? Then go out and enjoy doing those things now.

Soulution of the Day

Gather some people and start the I.C.S. — the International Carnival Society. Maybe the U.N. will accept it as a member.

GET TOUGH

When the going gets tough,
the tough get going.

— FRANK LEAHY

NORMAN VINCENT PEALE once shared something with me about surviving tough situations. He said when things were not going well, his mother always told him, "Norman, if God slams one door, further down the corridor another will be opened." With a mother like that, you can begin to see the light at the end of the tunnel.

Being tough isn't about being rough or rude but having the strength to meet any situation with an inner resource. Peale also shared that he had a fifth grade teacher who would write the word *can't* on the blackboard. He would then turn to the class, and they would tell him to erase the *'t,* leaving *can.*

Believe in yourself and see yourself as tough and able. Peale's teacher finished with, "You can if you think you can." We need to believe in our ability, our strength and toughness to survive and succeed. We need to believe that what we are doing is significant and meaningful. When we do, the ability to survive and be successful will be provided.

Soulution of the Day

Every time you think you can't, remove the t and you can.
Then use that t to get tough.

TITANIC

It is preoccupation with possessions,
more than anything else, that prevents us
from living freely and nobly.

— BERTRAND RUSSELL

HOW HARD IT IS FOR US to let go of the things we treasure. But how many of these things truly have value, and how many are simply objects we have accumulated?

If you were on the Titanic and had a life preserver in one hand and a bag of gold in the other, would you sink rather than let go of the gold? If your child didn't have a life preserver would you hold the gold or drop it and reach for your loved one? If only one of you could float with the preserver, what would you choose to let go of?

Sometimes it is the things we hang on to that pull us under and destroy our lives. We need to let go of the backpacks we carry that are full of garbage. When we let go of what is dragging us down, we are free of our burdens and can be lifted into the lifeboat. Why must we face the threat of being pulled under before we awaken to what keeps us afloat and what is significant in life?

There is more to surviving than indiscriminately hanging on. So define what you truly want to hold onto, and what gives your life meaning, and let go of the rest.

Soulution of the Day

Let go of what is pulling you under or draining your energy
so that you can keep your head above water.

MONEY

Money is to help make life easier.

— SIMON SIEGEL

ONE AFTERNOON I was speaking to a group called the Young Presidents' Association. It is made up of young men and women whose companies are worth millions of dollars. I asked them, "Is life fair?" Expecting to get a resounding yes as an answer, they yelled, "No," louder than any group I have ever spoken to. I answered, "It must be fair. You're all complaining."

Money doesn't solve your problems unless you know what to do with it. Ninety-five percent of all lottery winners say it ruined their lives five years after winning. My father, whom I quoted above, had his father die when he was twelve. He said it was one of the best things that ever happened to him. Why? Because it taught him how to survive on his own and to realize that money was to help make people's lives easier.

A while back one of our sons called me to ask for tuition money. I reminded him that he had received a good deal of money as an inheritance when my dad died. He said, "I gave it away to help a friend come to the States and go to college." I gave him the money grudgingly. I wasn't enlightened enough then to appreciate his exceptional act and how much like my father he was. I have learned from them both and can live a much happier and peaceful life not keeping track of who owes me what but instead looking for ways to help others in need.

When my family and I were robbed, instead of holding the anger, I learned to see myself as offering the thief a few more dollars to get his children or mother a wonderful Christmas or birthday present. Am I nuts? Sure, but they no longer are stealing the value of my life by controlling my thoughts and emotions.

Soulution of the Day

If you can't take it with you when you go, then give it away before you leave.

SANCTUARY

*Sanctuary... gives more than refuge
and release; it gives renewal.*

— MARGARET BLAIR JOHNSTONE

IF YOU NEED TIME TO REST and renew yourself, creating a sanctuary might be helpful. I often ask workshop participants how they would feel in a white room. Those who feel comfortable with it may find the image a useful place free of stimulation that they can use as a sanctuary. Similar to the Sabbath, a sanctuary offers you a chance to rest and do another kind of work — inner work, done in a place free of distractions.

You can create a sanctuary anywhere. You only have to close a door and enjoy pleasant aromas, sounds, and sights. You can create this with an aromatic candle, a painting or scene on the wall, and playing some quieting music. All you need to do is to close the door and let people know that you are taking "sanctuary time."

In your sanctuary, give yourself the gift of quiet time. Take the phone off the hook, turn off all appliances, radios, and televisions. Most of all, turn off your mind and bring peace home. Be still and know.

Soulution of the Day

*You do not need to leave the room you are sitting in to create a sanctuary.
It can be a real place or one in your mind, your corner of the universe.*

WARS

We have met the enemy and he is us.

— POGO

WHAT ARE WE TRYING TO KILL OR ELIMINATE? Why make war? I believe there are very few legitimate reasons to kill others. FBI agents are asked during their training if they could kill. Soldiers know they are being asked to go to war and kill other human beings. The question of whether it is okay to kill or go to war is a difficult one to answer.

In most cases, I believe, we are projecting onto others all the negative qualities we wish didn't exist within ourselves. So we strive to kill what we can't accept, causing ourselves and others great suffering. We go to war in the outer world because we can't face the war in our inner world. The internal war is even more painful, yet it is the true war we all face.

We must seek out the enemy within and destroy it. When we do, we will be able to help others do the same in their lives and stop being destructive toward one another. When we learn to love ourselves more than we hate our enemy, wars will cease.

Soulution of the Day

Be a courageous warrior and go within to defeat the true enemy.

GOOD THINGS

Unshared joy is an unlighted candle.

— SPANISH PROVERB

WE NEED TO BE MORE AWARE of how we communicate with each other. What would the world be like if when we met we only talked about the good things and recalled the positive about each other? We would look forward to meeting people we knew because we would each say, "I know something good about you" or "I heard some wonderful things about you."

What do we usually talk about when we meet? Most often our conversations center on our troubles and who or what caused them. We may even dream about them and devote a great deal of time to them — time we can't replace. We are all so aware of each other's deficits, inadequacies, and problems, when what we really need to focus on is the positive.

When we approach others in this positive way, it opens the door for them to feel better about themselves and offers an opportunity for us all to share joy.

Soulution of the Day

Start every conversation with, "I know something good about you"
or "I heard about something you did that was nice." See what happens.

GUARANTEED ON DUTY

A mighty fortress is our God,
a bulwark never failing.

— **MARTIN LUTHER**

IT OCCURRED TO ME THE OTHER DAY to put a sign at the foot of our driveway that said, "This home is protected by G.O.D." Our family has a contract with G.O.D. — Guaranteed on Duty security systems. I thought this would get everyone's attention. I wanted to let them know our home and possessions were protected by more than an alarm system, and that they too could have the same security at very little cost to the homeowner.

I believe the only true security one can have comes from a relationship with God. I cannot put into words what happens at the moment God comes into our life, but I have seen people cured of life-threatening illnesses when they "left their troubles to God." The closest I can come to describing it is the feeling of total serenity and peace of mind that comes from knowing you are never alone when facing life's difficulties.

A verse from *Amazing Grace* reflects my view and is the motto of our home security system as well: "The Lord has promised good to me. His word my faith secures. He will my shield and portion be as long as life endures."

Soulution of the Day

Sign on for a trial period with the G.O.D security system
and see what happens.

NEW IDEAS

*There is nothing more difficult
to take in hand, more perilous to conduct,
or more uncertain in its success, than to
take the lead in the introduction
of a new order of things.*

— NICCOLO MACHIAVELLI

WHEN I BEGAN SPEAKING at medical conferences about my experience with cancer patients and the relationship between mind and matter, the reaction of other doctors was a surprise. They started yelling at me. I even remember one asking me at the end of a conference, "Are you telling us we are doing it wrong?"

I have found that closed minds want to hear nothing new and fight back if you introduce them to new concepts. It is as if you are shattering their long-held beliefs, whether they be religious or scientific. No one wants to help you prove what they don't believe. They may even seek success by trying to prove, through research, that you are wrong. When their research shows you are right, they are in big trouble unless they then claim to have discovered what you were talking about in the first place.

Knowledge is an interesting thing to the open-minded and a problem to others. Seeing is not always believing, trust me. Even when others have seen the truth placed before their eyes, if it is not part of their belief system they deny it and claim the study was poorly controlled or find other excuses.

It is always a risk to share new ideas, but without them there would be no progress or growth.

Soulution of the Day

*Those who speak the truth must have the strength to tell
what they have experienced until it is accepted.
Be patient; the truth will become self-evident.*

WHY SLEEP?

The dreams of night prepare you
for the day that follows.

— LUCY, *PEANUTS*

WHY DO WE SLEEP? Do Lucy and Shakespeare, who wrote, "To sleep, perchance to dream," know something?

Most living things do not sleep the way we do. Horses sleep on their feet for only a few hours because they are aware that sleeping is a dangerous practice. Predators sleep longer because they have less to fear. Think back to a time when we slept in open areas easy for predators to get to. If you wanted to survive, you stayed awake or had someone stand guard. So why has evolution given us this need? I feel it is not simply because our bodies need a rest. Resting can be done without sleeping.

I believe we sleep to allow our conscious and unconscious minds to communicate and organize the wisdom that we are to be aware of. This wisdom, from our Creator, is communicated to us in dreams and visions. That is the universal language that creation speaks to us all. Different languages separate us, but symbols unite us.

When Charlie Brown asks Lucy what the above quote means, Lucy replies, "It's at night, Charlie Brown, that your brain is really working. Your brain is trying to sort everything out for you. It's trying to make you see yourself as you really are."

Soulution of the Day

Get a good night's sleep and dream away!

LIGHTBULB

*With all your science can you tell
how it is, and whence it is, that light
comes into the soul?*

— HENRY DAVID THOREAU

ARE YOU THE LIGHT OR THE BULB? Bulbs don't last forever. With time they burn out or break. But light goes on indefinitely; it can't burn out and has no limits. When you connect with the light within you, you touch infinity.

Don't be just the bulb being turned on and off at the request of others who flip your switch. You will not last long that way. You need time to meet your needs and just turn off and cool down, so you can reconnect with your inner light.

When you shine your light for others, they will learn from you and follow your illuminated path.

Soulution of the Day

*Don't let others flip your switch. Radiate your true light
and share the enlightenment.*

PRESCRIPTION #212

SWEETHEART

The small courtesies sweeten life;
the greater ennoble it.

— CHRISTIAN NESTELL BOVEE

MY WIFE CALLED ME "sweetheart" a few minutes ago, as she came into the room where I was working. I teased her by asking, "Why are you calling me sweetheart?"

"Because you are," she answered.

The beauty of the word really came through to me for the first time. For someone to be a sweetheart in your life is an incredible gift. We are more often dealing with broken hearts and chest pains instead of something that sweetens the life experience of the heart.

A life full of sweethearts would be good for anyone's health. Stop and think about all the people in your life who are your sweethearts, and notice how your body feels when you do this. If you can't think of anyone, don't blame the world. Take responsibility and go sweeten some hearts for your sake and theirs.

Soulution of the Day

See how many people you can be a sweetheart to today,
and remember, no artificial sweeteners allowed.

SUN AND SON

She had made the best of time
and time returned the compliment.

— LORD BYRON

I NOTICE THAT THE SUN RISES every morning with nary a complaint. Day after day it's up at the crack of dawn, spreading the light no matter what the weather conditions are. Our son gets up much later and still has many complaints and problems about himself and the world he encounters.

What is the difference between what the sun sees and what our son sees? One looks to spread the light and asks for nothing but the chance to contribute to the growth of life and to bring people a cheerful day. Our son is constantly looking for a better life for himself where the things that disturb him will no longer exist.

The sun has been around a lot longer and knows the right way to have a day of happiness. Our son is still learning, through his problems and feelings, how to find happiness in the new day. We each have that choice. We can bring more light or dark to the world by our choice each morning.

Soulution of the Day

Do you choose to bring the light or the clouds?
Choose to be a source of sunshine for someone today.

HOTEL STAYS

A comic says funny things,
and a comedian says things funny.

— MILTON BERLE

WHEN I ARRIVE AT A HOTEL I love to fill out the registration form and play with answers to the questions. It's the child, comic, multiple personality, comedian in me that takes over.

The first one asked is usually, *How long will you be staying with us?* I answer with, "I hope to have a long life. I have good genes, no health problems, and exercise regularly." The next line says *firm*. So I ask the clerk to give me a squeeze and tell me what to put down based upon her evaluation. *Company* comes next. I write yes, my wife. Then comes *employed by,* followed by a blank, which I usually fill in with *God*.

The question I love best occurs when I leave the room and forget my key. I go up to the desk to ask for another one and they ask, "Do you have identification?" I roll up a pant leg, then put my leg on the counter, and say, "This is a distinguishing birthmark." The person behind the counter usually backs off and calls my room. When the clerk bursts into a laugh, I know my wife has just told them to look for my birthmark to identify me.

I get a key and a smile, and they don't forget me no matter how long I stay.

Soulution of the Day

Always let your multiple personalities have a little fun too.
And always ask the clerk, "How can I help you?"

WALLS

*I get tired, just every now and then,
of beating my head against certain walls
that people and I build between
people and me.*

— ANONYMOUS

OUR CONNECTIONS AND RELATIONSHIPS keep us alive by giving our lives meaning. So why do we build walls around ourselves? I believe it is out of fear: what will others think if they see me, my home, my life, and what I am doing?

Walls keep us from seeing the truth and knowing one another. We cannot become one family if walls separate us. Break down the walls by coming out from behind yours and letting people know you. You can start with a small crack and by removing a few stones. When you see the benefit of revealing yourself, it will become easier to take the entire wall down. Until you have removed the separation, you will never know the people on the other side of the wall.

But if you're not quite ready to take the whole wall down, at least build it out of glass. That way you can both feel safe and still be able to see each other's truth. After a while there will be no need for a wall.

Soulution of the Day

Be a wall buster rather than a wall builder.

HARVEST

*To exist is to change;
to change is to mature; to mature
is to create oneself endlessly.*

— HENRI BERGSON

WE PLANT A SEED. It grows through the summer until harvest time arrives, and then we cut down what has grown. The roots remain, and the next spring the plant sprouts again. So it is with life. Death cuts us all down at some point. For some, the growing season is longer and we create ourselves many times over, but inevitably harvest time comes for all of us.

However, if we have established healthy roots firmly in the earth we are immortal. I see this when our family gets together and four generations seat themselves in the same room. It is an incredible feeling to realize that everyone in the room is connected to my parents through their children and their children's children. The roots have spread deep and wide over the earth and will forever sprout as long as life exists on this planet.

Your roots do not have to be related to the act of giving birth to a child, but to the active process of helping others to grow and thrive throughout the seasons of their life. You can be the farmer who provides the field and the sustenance so that others are able to put down their roots in your field of dreams.

Soulution of the Day

*Prepare your crop well so that at harvest time it will be ready to be
cut down and you will know the roots are strong and will continue to grow.*

ERRAND

*We are called upon not to be successful,
but to be faithful.*

— MOTHER TERESA

WE ARE ALL ON AN ERRAND for humanity. We are not sent here to destroy, but to build and create. We have to ask ourselves how our individual presence can change the course of humanity for the good.

If we change, humanity changes. It is not necessary to be the CEO of a major company or the president or prime minister of a powerful country to complete this errand. We just have to look at what is before us and start right where we are. We need to see where we can help, and then act in a way that fulfills our personal errand for humanity.

Every act has its effects, from tossing garbage on the roadside to loving thy neighbor. When you make a decision or take an action, ask yourself, "How will this affect humanity?"

Soulution of the Day

How do you plan to fulfill your errand to humanity?

BLESSINGS

*How often we are told what God
can do for us; how rarely what God can do
with us! God is now sort of a cosmic bellboy,
ready to do anything to make life pleasant
and safe without asking for anything more
than a reasonable tip.*

— WILLIAM SLOAN COFFIN

MOST OFTEN IN PRAYER we ask for what we want for ourselves and others. Yet studies done by quantum physicists show that prayers asking simply for blessings do more good than those asking for specific events to occur.

When we pray, how often do we offer ourselves as the bellboy or servant of the Creator? We need to seek harmony and not control. Creation is an ongoing process, and we cannot be placing orders every day based on our moods or desires. Blessings help us all. They provide an energy and state of mind that help us survive what life presents.

If all of creation was blessed, then problems would disappear, and everything we want would come to be.

Soulution of the Day

Try asking for blessings rather than specific things, and see what happens.

THE PEACEFUL DINOSAUR

When the power of love overcomes
the love of power the world will know peace.

— JIMI HENDRIX

I SAW THE COMPLETE SKELETON of a brontosaurus the other day. One thighbone weighed over five hundred pounds. Yet this enormous creature was probably a very gentle soul. Because of its weight it spent a lot of time in the water and survived by eating enormous amounts of soft greens that grew there.

We are so small next to a brontosaurus, yet look at how destructive we can be. How does one make sense out of it all? Why is our little species into killing each other and many other forms of life, while the enormous brontosaurus was only interested in eating greens?

I know there were aggressive dinosaurs that killed other dinosaurs, and I accept the fact that nature requires a cycle of life and death to sustain itself. But why does humankind choose to destroy? The bigger we get, the more we threaten others with our power. I do not have a quick and easy solution. I do know that dinosaurs have come and gone, and we will be gone too unless we change our way of living and choose to live in peace and not conflict.

Soulution of the Day

You have the power to make a difference.
Choose love and peace.

LOTTERY WINNER

What happens to a man is less significant than what happens within him.

— Louis L. Mann

I PLAY THE LOTTERY REGULARLY in the hopes of winning and doing some good in the world with the funds I receive. Very few of the things I would think of spending the money on are for personal reasons.

Yet I realized the other day that I have already won the lottery! For me the real lottery is about my life and family, the love we all share, and the things we have done and will do for others. That is of far greater value than any cash that may come my way from a winning lottery ticket. To look around at generations of my family and feel the love and know the kindness of these people is to be and feel like a winner.

The majority of families who win the lottery find it to be one more reason to fight and argue over who deserves what. In our family we all share equally and have the children's welfare at heart. We are all winners, a wonderful feeling. Give it a try. Try seeing all the ways in which you are a winner.

Soulution of the Day

Win the lottery of life and share your love and winnings.

ANGER

That's what happens when you're angry at people. You make them part of your life.

— GARRISON KEILLOR

I THINK THERE ARE TIMES when anger is appropriate, such as when you are not treated with respect. When you cannot release anger, it hurts you more than the person you are angry at. When you cannot let go of bitterness, resentment, and aggravation over whatever has happened, then you allow it to continue to damage your life.

Your thoughts are what control the outcome. Read letters to the editors of daily papers, and you will learn what bothers everyone. Rarely do you see a letter expressing thanks or reflecting on a pleasant experience. By your anger you make clear who you are and what you believe in.

Almost invariably, people's unhealthy anger is about principles and rules of behavior that they are having trouble with. The best advice I can give is this: stop writing angry letters about what a good person should do, and be one instead. Stop criticizing, and be the person you wish everyone else to be.

Soulution of the Day

Right beliefs are one thing, but right action is everything.

WHAT IS A MIRACLE?

There are only two ways to live your life.
One is as though nothing is a miracle.
The other is as though everything is a miracle.

— **ALBERT EINSTEIN**

WHILE I WAS READING the other night, I came across this question: "What is a miracle?" It made me think about the things in our lives that my mother called "God's Redirections." She used this term for the seemingly random incidents that affect our lives in a positive way.

Maybe it is the person you happen to meet, what you accidentally pick up to read, the help that comes unexpectedly from strangers, or one of a million other possibilities that bring miracles to our lives. Perhaps these seemingly random incidents are more than they appear to be. Perhaps these are the real miracles!

Soulution of the Day

We just need to recognize that the potential
for miracles is present all the time.

PRESCRIPTION #223

LOVE BLINDNESS

*Love isn't blind; it just only sees
what matters.*

— WILLIAM CURRY

WHAT MAKES A LOVER BLIND? What is it a lover can't see? Is blindness always a bad thing?

What do you see when you start the day and step into your living room? Is the first thing you see the mess from the night before and what has to be done, or the potential for the day ahead?

Wake up to life and start looking at what is before you. You can select what you are blind to. Loving life and being blind to its faults and problems does not mean you aren't aware of them. It does not prohibit you from trying to change things for the better. But it does mean you are not controlled by them and made bitter and resentful by them.

When you are in the slowest line at the checkout counter and the clerk stops to page the manager after you have already emptied your cart onto the belt, and you are ready to scream, use your love blindness. See through loving eyes and watch what happens to your sight.

Soulution of the Day

*Spread the affliction of love blindness
and hope that people don't find a cure.*

SACRED SPACE

The modern world has sought to deny the sacredness of human life. But it has not denied it absolutely. Rather, it has distorted it. It has not done away with the notion of sacredness altogether. It has merely replaced it with relatively superficial notions such as the "quality of life."

— DONALD DEMARCO

WHEN I FIRST SEE the words *sacred space* I think of temples and shrines around the world. I think of special places in my own home. But when I pause to think, I realize the most sacred place is within each of us. We are sacred things, and yet how many of us treat ourselves that way?

Do we stop to think about our bodies as sacred places? A sacred place is honored and kept clean, touched with reverence so as not to mar or injure it. Sometimes it is a storage place for significant and meaningful events and objects. How many of us treat our bodies as such?

Why do we abuse our sacred bodies with poisons both physical and emotional? I think it is because so few of us have ever been treated as sacred. When we are treated and seen as imperfect objects to be scorned, we cannot see the sacredness within us.

Remember, you are a child of God. If someone treats you badly, it is their problem; they have no sacred space in their minds, bodies, or lives from which to view your divinity.

Soulution of the Day

Create a sacred space in your life from which to honor the holy within you and others.

DIRECTIONS

*If the lost traveler really needs only to
slow down, pull out a map and
take a moment to figure out where he is...
can those of us who've lost our direction
in life do the same?*

— DEBORAH NORVILLE

WHEN I GO OUT JOGGING or bike riding, I often get stopped by
people who need directions to some place in the area. I don't pay
attention to street names, and so I find it hard to give accurate
directions. I started carrying a map in my pocket so I would be able
to give them more specific instructions.

The other day a woman pulled up, and I was ready to get out
my map when she said, "I have cancer and could use your help."
She needed directions too — just a different kind.

We all need help finding our way, or so I have come to learn.
Many religions and philosophies use the words *path, direction, gate,*
or *the way* as part of their message. I don't think of these words as
related to any map but to the direction of our lives. There are
mountains to climb and rivers to cross if we are to get where we
need to be.

Soulution of the Day

*There is nothing wrong with asking for help and directions,
but only you can decide on your destination.*

WORKAHOLIC

*If it frustrates you that they
don't allow laptops on a Ferris wheel,
you may be a workaholic.*

— DR. DONALD E. WETMORE

PICASSO TALKED ABOUT the difference between being a workaholic and a productive person. Ask yourself whether you find time for creativity and play. If the answer is no, perhaps you are a workaholic. Next, ask yourself if what you are doing separates you from people or brings them into your life. If you are creative your work will bring people to you, while the workaholic has no time for people. Why would anyone want to be a workaholic? Be brave and ask that of yourself.

If you were brought up on self-destructive mottos with workaholic parents, then that is the pattern you see as the appropriate choice, even when it isn't. Wake up to the creative and playful child inside of you. Give it some freedom to express itself and enjoy the world rather than being separated from it.

Soulution of the Day

*Make a list with two columns. At the top of one put "productive"
and at the top of the other put "workaholic." Now list a typical
day's activities. Which side do you lean toward?*

PRESCRIPTION #227

SPIRIT GUIDES

*Be open to all teachers, and all teachings,
and listen with your heart.*

— RAM DASS

MANY YEARS AGO I attended a workshop run by Elisabeth
Kübler-Ross and listened to her talk about the spirits and guides we
all have around to help us. Another surgeon there had his doubts,
but I was open to her words and experience. When I went home
and began to live what she said, I was converted.

There have been many times in my life when my belief in
spirits and guides has been confirmed. One time I was standing
alone in a hallway after delivering a Sunday sermon at a friend's
funeral when Olga Worrall, a spiritual healer, walked over and
asked me if I was Jewish. I thought she was confused by my speaking at the Sunday service. "Why do you ask?" I said.

"Because," she said, "there are two rabbis standing next to you."
She went on to tell me their names and what they were wearing.
Her description was exactly what I had seen in my meditations.

One night while I was giving a lecture, I noticed that the words
coming out of me had no relationship to my notes. It felt like I was
not the one creating the speech, but was being used to deliver it. At
the end, a woman came up and told me that I was better than usual
and that a man was standing in front of me during the entire
lecture. She said, "I drew his picture. Here it is." It still hangs in my
home, and again I knew exactly who it was: my inner guide. Since
then I let him do all the work.

Soulution of the Day

*We all have guidance and help available
through the field of consciousness.*

INFERIORITY COMPLEX

Everyone who succeeds does so because of an inferiority complex. Fortunately, everyone has an inferiority complex.

— MARIE BEYNON RAY

YOU CAN SEE THE THINGS in your life that you feel inferior about either as assets or as liabilities. If you accept the fact that you are inferior, you will never change. You will become comfortable in that role. There is no risk involved in being inferior or incapable of doing something. Everyone will leave you alone and not ask for your help or participation in projects.

But when you review the lives of the most well known artists, athletes, politicians, and other successful people, you will find it was their inferiority that motivated them to change. They didn't just go from being inferior to average. They were determined to excel and put in the effort and energy required.

So look at yourself and decide what you feel inferior about and change it. I never see our pets having any problems with feeling inferior. So it must be something that has developed in us because of our nature or how we treat each other and measure ourselves and our successes. If we have created it, it is something we can change.

Soulution of the Day

Notice when you feel inferior.
Define it, and then succeed because of it.

SHOW DOG SHOW

I think dogs are the most amazing creatures;
they give unconditional love. For me they are
the role model for being alive.

— GILDA RADNER

MY WIFE AND I were just watching the Westminster Dog Show. They had a wonderful short segment about what we can learn from dogs. This reminded me of something I use at my lectures. I always read a list that asks: Can you do without caffeine, eat the same food every day, judge all people the same, not bore people with your troubles, accept criticism without resentment? and so on. Then I end it with, "If so, you're almost as good as your dog."

People have no idea that these questions will end that way because I read them in all seriousness. They laugh, but it isn't really funny. I didn't have time to copy the list of dog qualities from the TV segment, but they also talked about greeting people with enthusiasm, making up after disagreements, taking a relaxing walk, and enjoying the moment.

That is why I entitled this prescription "Show Dog Show." There are "show dogs" that feature qualities of the breed, and there are "dog shows" — those dogs that show us how we ought to behave. Dogs are great teachers that remind us how we ought to be living to make this a friendlier planet. A dog growl is one thing, but what people do to each other quite another.

Soulution of the Day

Watch a dog show and learn something.

WINGED MESSENGERS

Death is not a period,
but a comma, in the story of life.

— ANONYMOUS

I HAVE HEARD MANY STORIES while leading groups for the bereaved that have convinced even a skeptical scientist like me that we continue to receive messages from our loved ones even after death.

At one group a woman shared how her daughter, who was murdered, loved birds. She went on to tell how at her other daughter's outdoor wedding a bird had interrupted the service. All the guests there knew it was her dead sister saying hello. Just as she finished telling us her story, a bird flew into our meeting room through an open window. It was the only time that ever had happened in all the years we had met there. Of course everyone said, "It's your daughter."

Another time, a woman shared that one winter she was driving down the highway when her son's favorite bird, a seagull, landed on the highway in front of her. She felt it was her son wanting her to stop. She did, and then resumed driving. When she went to make the next turn, she realized that the road was covered with ice and many cars had skidded and collided with each other. She realized that if she hadn't stopped she would have crashed right into them.

I believe there is no time or space after we leave our bodies, so we can continue to communicate with those we love.

Soulution of the Day

Be open-minded and notice and receive messages from those
who have passed on. Do not let your limiting beliefs block your ability to
experience a more expansive reality.

TREES

*The trees in the storm don't try to stand up
straight and tall and erect. They allow themselves to bend and be blown with the wind.
They understand the power of letting go.
Those trees and those branches that try too
hard to stand up strong and straight
are the ones that break.*

— JULIA BUTTERFLY HILL

WE ALL NEED TO KNOW either how to bend or how to become strong enough to resist breaking when one of life's storms confronts us. However, if neither of those possibilities is available, we need to appreciate what Hemingway said, that if you do break you can become strong at the broken places.

Fractured bones are stronger at the healed fracture site than are normal bones. Life is like that. If we learn from whatever breaks us apart, we can become stronger and not break down when problems confront us.

The same goes with personality. The egotistical, inflated, and stubborn become uprooted and knocked over trying to prove how tough they are. Be willing to bend and give when forces beyond your control challenge you. Then when things quiet down you can recover and move on with your life. Ultimately your experiences will make you strong enough to resist many things other people can't. But until then let go, stop trying to prove something, bend, and go with the wind.

Soulution of the Day

*Think of life as an exercise program. The more flexible you become
and the more you work things out, the stronger you will become.*

SING

He who sings frightens away his ills.
— MIGUEL DE CERVANTES, *DON QUIXOTE*

NO ONE IN MY FAMILY WAS VERY MUSICAL. Oh, we all sang, but no one knew whether or not they were on key because we were all basically tone deaf. My wife's mom, however, was an opera singer. When I started to date Bobbie, who is never on time, I would sit at their living room piano and with one finger play a song and sing. I noticed that her mother always shut the windows while I sang. When it became obvious that her daughter and I were getting serious, she told me the pain I was causing the family with my singing.

A friend of mine is a guitarist and he offered to accompany me when I sang *Amazing Grace* at the end of a retreat for cancer patients. At lunch he said, "Sing a few lines for me." I did, and he played along. That evening as I sang I could hear him playing, and it sounded awful. I asked if I had sung in a different key, and he said, "You sang in several keys. That was the problem."

After many years of my wife's coaching, I can hear the music and sing on key most of the time. So she actually enjoys my singing now. The point of all this is that we should all sing our own song. It is therapeutic to sing and, I will add, if you are off-key don't worry, just sing in the car and the shower.

Soulution of the Day

So just like the song says, sing, sing your song,
don't worry if it's not good enough, just sing.

WHOLENESS

*Moments of holiness happen
when we experience moments of
wholeness with ourselves.*

— ANONYMOUS

THE ROOT OF THE WORD *integrity* means the quality of being complete or unbroken, or wholeness.

When are we whole? What does the word mean to you? For me, it is not about my body but a sense of who I am. It is about my essence, regardless of how many body parts may be missing or the condition of those present. My wholeness is about my integrity as a human being. It is about my ability to love and be honest, my willingness to feel and even suffer. It is about my being real to all those with whom I have relationships and being willing to look at the aspects of myself that I do not feel comfortable with.

To be whole is to be complete. To be complete is not just about our physical parts but about being a complete human being, one who fulfills his or her part in the nature of life.

Soulution of the Day

What makes you feel whole and complete?

READ IT ALOUD

What kind of man deserves the most pity?
A lonesome man on a rainy day who
does not know how to read.

— BENJAMIN FRANKLIN

A FRIEND OF MINE NAMED GLORIA puts out a daily email called *Heaven Letters*. When I read it I sometimes become critical of her writing style and the words she uses to express some very meaningful and spiritual concepts. My mind wants to focus on the literal content rather than on the underlying meaning. She recently made a CD of the same material, and I love listening to her read it. I don't find myself being so analytical when I listen to her voice. The material seems much more profound when I hear it.

The actor Charles Laughton was accused by a member of the audience of editing one of Shakespeare's plays when he read it aloud. The man said it was the first time he ever understood Shakespeare, and that's why he thought it was edited. What can we learn from all this? Try reading aloud to yourself and your family and anyone else who will listen. Your display of emotion changes the words, and people will listen more attentively.

I have also learned to reread the same books and plays aloud as a test of my growth. If the reading becomes boring, I know I have not progressed in my development. But when each reading presents me with new ideas and bits of wisdom I did not notice before, I know I am growing and opening my mind and life to new things.

Soulution of the Day

Read, and listen to audio versions of the same book or lecture,
and if the speaker seems to become wiser each time, you are doing well.

REFLECTION AND AFFECTION

We are disturbed not by things,
but by the view which we take of them.

— EPICTETUS

A WHILE BACK ONE OF OUR CATS and I stood before the mirror. The cat, named Miracle, seemed not at all concerned with the condition of her fur coat, her crooked tail, or other physical defects. She just looked at herself and made no requests for a brushing, shampoo, or plastic surgery.

I looked at myself and was not quite as happy with my body. I felt it could use some changes. But I guess I am not up to making the ones that would make a difference, and I am not one for plastic surgery. I admired Miracle's attitude and tried to learn from her instead.

My sense is that she accepts herself, and I have trouble doing that. I want to be able to look in the mirror someday and just say, "Hi, it's me" to my body the way Miracle does. Hopefully, with practice, one day I will be able to do just that.

Soulution of the Day

Every day greet your reflection with affection and acceptance.

LAUGH LASTS

A smile increases your face value.
Laughter is contagious; be a carrier.
He who laughs, lasts!

— Adages used by Bobbie Siegel

Your thoughts lead to your feelings, and your feelings affect your body chemistry. When you laugh and smile it has a positive, healing effect on your body.

When my wife, Bobbie, does her stand-up comedy routine, I see the uplifting effect it has on the audience. No one ever complains about the time you spend making them laugh or exposing them to love. Emails filled with humor are sent to us all, and we usually don't think of them as spam.

Laugh, smile; it is therapeutic. Since you are only on the planet for a limited time, then why take it so seriously? Yes, I know we have problems, and I do not mean to play down the fact that there are those who are starving and homeless. But do you think they are ever upset with someone who makes them laugh? Laughter is always good medicine, even when times are difficult.

Soulution of the Day

Be a comedian, according to your talents,
and help people find a reason to smile.

CREATIVITY

It is something one does alone...and to recognize and accept that, and stop asking how, is to take the first step in our own creativity.

— MICHAEL DRURY

HAVE YOU EVER STOPPED to think that God didn't have a blueprint for creation? Though we complain about life's imperfections and difficulties, let's be honest, God did a Heaven of a job, considering.

We are all creators; we just need to tap into that divine place within ourselves that inspires us. When you know yourself and what you desire, you will be creative too. You will be compelled to do whatever it will take to accomplish your goal. You won't ask how, you will just do.

After a concert a woman once rushed up to violinist Fritz Kreisler exclaiming, "I'd give my life to play as you do!" Kreisler answered somberly, "I did."

Soulution of the Day

What would you like to create?
Be yourself and have the courage to create.
If you get tired take a day of rest. Our Creator did.

MY BEST DAY

Life needs to be appreciated
more than it needs to be understood.

— STUART HELLER

ONE DAY AT THE BANK when it was my turn to approach the teller, I asked, "What's the best day of your life?" She paused a moment and then responded, "When I gave birth to my daughter." A voice from across the bank called out, "Wrong." Then there was a discussion about how someone could tell her that she was wrong. Before it became too heated I interrupted to say, "The best day of your life, and everyone's life, is today. Don't forget that and live it. It is the only day you have."

I find it very easy to carry out therapy in the bank by asking the tellers questions. Sometimes I just say, "How may I help you?" when I get to the window. I also love to go to the drive-up window at the bank and ask, "Is my order ready?" They all know it's me. When I call the office where our son, the attorney, works and tell the secretary I am an FBI agent, our son always answers the phone with, "Yes, Dad, what is it?" His secretary knows now.

If you think that's crazy, I once called the outpatient operating room through the parking garage door intercom, where people enter to pick up post-op patients. There is a ramp there for wheel-chairs. I didn't identify myself; I just said, "I need someone to hold the door so I can drive my VW in and pick up a patient." I heard a secretary shriek in fear. Then a moment later I heard a nurse's voice say, "We'll be there to help in a minute, Dr. Siegel."

Soulution of the Day

Lighten up and have your best day ever, daily.

ETERNAL TRUTHS

Truth is by nature self-evident.
As soon as you remove the cobwebs
of ignorance that surround it,
it shines clear.

— MOHANDAS GANDHI

THE TRUTH IS, there is nothing to say or learn that those who have preceded us haven't already said or learned. Wise people and teachers have always expressed the same things, because life's difficulties and life's truths do not change with time. I prefer to use the term the "wisdom of the sages" to refer to these teachings.

I do not deny that it is helpful to publish their wisdom in many languages and stories that are modernized and easier to understand. Each of us knows the truths deep inside; it is our path in life to reconnect with them, thus diminishing our suffering and increasing our joy.

We tend to rediscover, through our personal fortunes and misfortunes, the eternal truths that have been taught by the prophets of the past. Whether it is winning the lottery or acquiring a life-threatening disease, every experience holds a lesson to bring us closer to the eternal truths.

Soulution of the Day

May the day come when we are all aware of
and practice these eternal truths.

GOOD-BYE

*Friendship and community are,
first of all, inner qualities.*

— HENRI NOUWEN

WHEN YOU SAY the word *good-bye,* what are you feeling and thinking? Do you want to be separated from the other person, the "good-bye and good riddance" feeling, or do you want to remain connected even when apart?

Good-byes can be bridge builders that keep us connected even when we are apart. In some ways they maintain a spiritual and emotional tie between you and the person you said good-bye to. Think about your intentions when you say good-bye, and you will be able to remain in touch with the people you relate to in the world, no matter how far apart you are.

We have to remember that consciousness is not local, and when we wish goodness for others we help it to happen. Keep others in your thoughts and prayers and help them to experience a good-bye. Good things are more likely to come to them because of how you act after you say good-bye.

Soulution of the Day

*Build bridges with your words and thoughts,
and that will keep you connected to the people in your life.*

TREE OF LIFE

Stand Tall & Proud
Remember your Roots!
Be content with your Natural Beauty
Drink Plenty of Water
Enjoy the View!

— **ILLAN SHAMIR,** *ADVICE FROM A TREE*

IF WE ARE BUSILY performing deeds but never stop to reach up for knowledge and wisdom, our tree of life will have no branches and many roots. Without branches, how can it move and respond with the winds of life? Or if we accumulate great knowledge but perform no deeds, then we are like a tree with many branches but no roots, and we will be blown over by the winds of fortune.

We must see that our tree of life contains both wisdom and deeds. Then our branches will spread and our deep roots will provide support and nourishment. We will be able to survive the storms and droughts that life presents us.

Soulution of the Day

Is your tree of life blossoming and secure,
or do you need to put down more roots or grow more branches?

THE SHEPHERD

All the children are my sheep,
no matter the color of their wool.

— KNUTE SHMEDLEY

I WAS NAMED AFTER my father's father. He died of tuberculosis when my dad was a child. Bernard was my given name. I was born in the Jewish Hospital in Brooklyn, New York. When my folks were giving the information for the birth certificate, they said, "Bernard, son of Simon." The latter was said in Hebrew, and the man filling out the papers didn't admit his confusion, writing on the certificate "Shepard" as my middle name.

My folks were surprised when they saw this name on the certificate, but it has turned out to be appropriate. I believe that the work I have done and the things I have devoted my life to show that I was meant to be a shepherd (even if it's spelled Shepard). I do not think accidents are always accidents. Sometimes a wisdom manifests itself in ways we can't explain.

Call it what you will: coincidences, accidents, synchronicity. There is not always an obvious reason for the things that happen. We don't know all the answers and probably never will. We do need to pay attention, though, to the messages that come to us if we are to follow our intended path.

Soulution of the Day

Does your name in any way reveal who you really are?
Why do you think so?

DREAMS

*Trust the dreams, for in them
is hidden the gate to eternity.*

— KAHLIL GIBRAN

EVERYONE MUST HAVE A DREAM. Dreams are the universal language and the only way the future can express itself and be known to us. To not dream is to die. When you stop dreaming and being aware of your dreams, you are closing the door to the truth and to your potential life.

A wish and a dream are separate concepts. A wish is a conscious desire that may or may not come true, that is, unless you have a genie working for you who can guarantee you three wishes. A dream is a vision of what can be. If you focus on the vision you make changes in your life, both conscious and unconscious, that make the dream a reality.

The day you stop dreaming your life loses meaning. The dreamer lives an ageless life, always growing and changing to create the dreams she has dreamt. Even if your dream is never fulfilled, you will not regret having it. As Don Quixote said, "To dream the impossible dream" is the finest thing one can do.

Soulution of the Day

*Dream your possible and impossible dreams
and ride off into the sunset with your Sancho Panza beside you.*

ANDROGYNY

It is fatal to be a man or woman pure and simple: one must be a woman manly, or a man womanly.

— VIRGINIA WOOLF

ANIMA AND ANIMUS, female and male — why? Why not one sex with the ability to divide as a means of reproducing? Well, it wouldn't be as much fun, and comedians would have no material! Aside from that, I think there are other reasons. We need the balance to be complete, to understand ourselves, and to have much greater potential.

I see those who limit themselves to the "masculine" or "feminine" role only as missing out on a great deal in their lives. I don't mean your appearance as a male or female, but about developing as a person and being open to a wide range of emotions and abilities.

By encompassing both male and female, we are free to feel, see, and do things we never would have attempted otherwise. Look at the world and see the courage of women who do not limit themselves and are willing to compete with men. Look at the men who are not afraid to do the things that women are known for. They are willing to be their whole self and live a more fulfilled life. When we restrict each other in business, voting, and family and gender roles, we limit our full potential.

Soulution of the Day

Free yourself to become a whole person with a complete androgynous personality.

OLD WOUNDS

The old skin has to be shed
before the new one can come.

— JOSEPH CAMPBELL

WE ALL CARRY OLD WOUNDS within us; for some they are physical and for others they are emotional. There are many reasons why these wounds don't heal and why we continue to hold on to them. For some they offer a way of life that protects them from being whole and having to live a life with responsibilities. For others, the constant eating away of their body and soul by old wounds keeps them from healing.

The other night I dreamt of sewing up old wounds in many people. As a surgeon, I found this very interesting. I know it is related to what is happening in my life and my resolve to change my ways and help heal relationships with members of my family.

It also made me realize that it is never too late to close old wounds and start again as a whole human being, free of the hurts of the past. The possibility to heal is always there. We always have the freedom to choose healing. We don't have to live with the scars, injuries, and wounds of the past.

Soulution of the Day

Work on healing your old wounds,
and don't be afraid to ask others for help.

PRESCRIPTION #246

IMAGINE

*The courage to imagine
the otherwise is our greatest resource.*

— DANIEL J. BOORSTIN

WE ARE TOLD TO DREAM the impossible dream, but who knows what is impossible? Does it make sense to look at an enormous aircraft and think it can fly, not to mention to the moon? What are your unspoken dreams and imaginings? Write them down, and when you have time explore and develop them. If we never imagine what can be, it will never come into being.

When you imagine what your life could be like, you start the unconscious preparation for the change, and things begin to happen. When an inventor imagines or gets an idea, the world changes. We use so many things today and take for granted what others could never have imagined. Picture a caveman returning to earth and being told about flush toilets and microwave ovens.

Do not thwart your children's imaginations by being discouraging and telling them to get in touch with reality. Reality is what we imagine it to be. Your life and your accomplishments can only be what you imagine is in store for you as you create your life.

Soulution of the Day

Do as John Lennon wrote and "Imagine."

PRESCRIPTION #247

THE NEW AGE

Which would you rather have?
New Age... or No Age?

— MICK WINTER

WHAT DOES THE NEW AGE MEAN TO ME? It represents a "Let's open our eyes" attitude. Once the New Age held that the world was round, and no one was receptive to that. But just a short time later, it became common knowledge. There is always a New Age that represents what we are yet to discover.

If people can believe in and stay open to a new reality, then the world will slowly change. I think that is what the New Age is always about, because what is reality today can change tomorrow.

For instance, twenty years ago I was considered crazy for talking to people under anesthesia. Now, in the medical literature, articles show that if you talk to people under anesthesia they experience less pain and go home sooner. So suddenly my teachings are old hat. It's wonderful to be able to be a little crazy and stay open to the next New Age.

Soulution of the Day

Always be willing to move forward into the New Age.

POOREST GRADE

Let your heart guide you.
It whispers, so listen closely.

— FROM THE FILM
THE LAND BEFORE TIME

IN COLLEGE MY WORST GRADE was a *C* in Creative Writing. I was a pre-med science major trying to broaden my experience. But since I lived primarily in my head, I was so intellectual there was nothing creative about my writing. I could have let that so-called defeat keep me from ever writing again.

Years later a patient of mine, who is a psychic, told me I was going to write a book. I told her about my college experience and laughed. Of course she turned out to be right. Since then she has told me how many more books I am going to write, including this one. I have had several books on the best-seller list, and my words have spread all over the world through them.

Over the years I have learned to move from my head to my heart. My books are written from my heart, my experience, and my life. I recall reading one of William Saroyan's novels in which a writer, after reading a letter his assistant wrote to his father, compliments his assistant for his wonderful writing. The assistant denies he knows how to write and says, "It's only a letter to my father." The writer answers, "Then write a letter to everyone." That is what I have learned to do.

Soulution of the Day

In what area might a shift from head to heart open your creative avenues?

GOD'S LIFELINES

To mark a friend's remains these stones arise;
I never knew but one and here he lies.

— LORD BYRON

THE ABOVE QUOTE is inscribed on a monument erected to Lord Byron's dog, Boatswain. The epitaph describes the one whose remains lie nearby. He possessed "Beauty without vanity, strength without insolence, courage without ferocity, and all the virtues of man without his vices."

I am a lover of animals and children; we always had a house full of both. Adults, I have problems with sometimes. I try to remember they were once children too. A book of poetry I am reading basically says the same thing. A poem about a cat finishes with, "For the name of the kitten was love." I wish as humans we could have such unconditional love between us as we do with our pets.

The Bible tells us to learn from the animals, but when will the day come that we become better students?

Soulution of the Day

Dog *is* God *spelled backward,*
and lifeline *is three-fourths* feline. *Get the message?*

SONG OF LIFE

*You don't get harmony
when everybody sings the same note.*

— DOUG FLOYD

*The world didn't begin with a big bang,
But with a silence which was replaced by the symphony of life.
Each of us had the right to choose the instrument
By which we create our music
And serve to maintain the harmony.
We may all play different instruments
And make different sounds,
Some of which hurt our ears,
But when we are all playing the same tune,
In spite of our differences,
We are in harmony.
And, that tune is the song of songs
called Life.*

Soulution of the Day

*Join the universal orchestra: toot your horn,
sing your heart out, bang your drum, and harmonize.*

TIDES

Don't fight the river;
it flows on its own.

— ANONYMOUS

WE CAN FIGHT THE TIDE and get nowhere. Trying to move against the tide or swim upstream is ineffective. You are fighting the energy of nature, and it never works to fight against the forces of creation.

When you fight the forces of nature it is either because you are unwise or because you have desires you are unwilling to give up. So you fight the forces of life and get nowhere. Then you become bitter and resentful because life is not flowing the way you want it to.

Why not change the direction of the rudder of your desires, go with the tide, and have the wind at your back? It may not be the most direct way to get where you want to go, but you will be going with the flow of life and becoming a part of the process of creation rather than a force resisting nature.

Soulution of the Day

Use the forces nature provides and save your energy.

IT'S BITTER AND I DON'T LIKE IT

Suffering is not an elective;
it is a core course in the University of Life.

— STEVEN J. LAWSON

WE DO NOT SEEK MEANING, serenity, or answers when our life is stable and peaceful. We accept our good fortune and don't question our beliefs. But when life blesses us with afflictions, diseases, death, or loss, the search begins.

At workshops I ask if any participants wish they could be free of all pain, emotional or physical. If any answer yes, I give them my phone number should they decide to cancel their wish. Why would they do that? Pain is the unwanted gift that defines and protects us. You would literally lose parts of your body and ultimately your life if you were numb to all experiences. Yet our society promotes numbness in so many ways.

The bitter pill of grief and pain is what starts the search for your road to serenity. Taste the bitterness of life and feel the discomfort. Accept and learn from your pain, and it will lead you to a place of meaning and wisdom.

Soulution of the Day

Our afflictions are not imposed by the Divine.
Rather, they lead us to the Divine more often than our joys do.
Do not resist the bitter pills in your life;
know that they will lead you to a greater awareness.

PRESCRIPTION #253

FOR WHAT REASON

*There is occasions and causes
why and wherefore in all things.*

— WILLIAM SHAKESPEARE, *KING HENRY V*

THERE IS ALWAYS A REASON. Often that is hard to accept in the midst of troubled times. Even though the reason may not be apparent, it is still present. Sometimes we only learn the reason why long after the event occurs, and other times we may never know it and must trust that it is part of a divine plan.

In our hour of darkness, we sometimes wonder about a higher power or question God's wisdom. At other times we are so tied to our own ego perceptions of the situation that the true reason eludes us. When we become stuck in finding the reason, we are left feeling miserable and powerless. Only when we are willing to trust and see beyond ourselves can true learning and healing begin.

Soulution of the Day

*Reasons may not always be apparent,
so don't become caught in the search.*

LITTLE DICKENS

*If God is at the front door
the devil is at the back door.*

— C. G. JUNG

WE HAVE MANY CATS, all with symbolic names. One, as a kitten, was into all kinds of mischief, and I wanted to name him Devil. But my wife didn't like that name. Then one day I heard her say to him, "Come here, you little Dickens." That became his name. He, of course, turned into an angel after that.

The next cat we adopted I named Gabriel after the angel. Of course he is not terribly angelic in his demands, but I wanted the balance of the devil and the angel and to acknowledge their presence in our lives.

Within us and in society live the trickster, the court jester, and the little Dickens. When we acknowledge their presence in us and our lives, we remain in control of our behavior. When we deny them we act out and look for excuses for our behavior, and they make trouble for us. When you literally accept the possibility that you could become a criminal, it is far less likely you will become one.

Soulution of the Day

*Accept the "little Dickens" in you so your shadow
won't cause you any trouble!*

DECLARE AND DEVOTE

Make love, not war!

— ANTIWAR SLOGAN

WE FREQUENTLY HEAR our political leaders speaking about declaring war against other peoples and nations. They are very devoted to the process of conflict, war, getting even, punishing others in damaging ways. They are seemingly not in touch with the people who suffer because of these declarations and devotions.

What would happen if our leaders were to declare love and devote themselves not to changing and punishing others, but to caring for and loving them? You can read these lines and nod in approval, but what if the questions were asked of you? Have you declared war against friends or family members and devoted yourself to changing their bad habits through criticism and conflict? Well, if you want peace of mind and happiness in your life and in the world, declare love and devote yourself to other people's well-being rather than trying to change them.

Soulution of the Day

What will you declare, love or war?

CHAUFFEUR

*Being a good chauffeur is more than
just knowing how to drive.*

— ADELE RUTH

WHEN SOMEONE YOU CARE ABOUT is involved in a serious dilemma, be it physical or psychological, you can be his or her chauffeur. We chuckle about this at our therapy meetings because the husbands who come often introduce themselves as their wife's chauffeur. They are not there ready to share the emotional experience, but come as a mechanical aide to their wives.

One husband I know, Mike Tucchio, is sharing the trip with his wife and used the chauffeur as his metaphor in a beautiful poem:

*But I am separated from my wife's reality.
The cancer is in her body, not mine.
Like the glass that separates the limousine driver from the passenger.
The two occupants travel together, but I am only the chauffeur.*

He understands that he is there to help, but he is like a good chauffeur, following the directions that come from the back seat. Where they go isn't up to him. He has to let his passenger decide the route and the destination. He and his wife, Barbara, are a special team and know where they are going.

Soulution of the Day

*The next time you find yourself acting as a chauffeur,
remember to listen to the backseat driver.*

HOT OR COLD

*I learned that nothing is impossible
when we follow our inner guidance,
even when the direction may threaten us
by reversing our usual logic.*

— GERALD JAMPOLSKY

WHEN CHILDREN PLAY A GAME in which they have to find a hidden item or treasure, they are guided by the words *hot* and *cold*. If they are getting closer to the item they say you are getting warmer, and when very near you are hot. The opposite is true if they head off in the wrong direction; then they are getting colder.

Many people wish life presented us with a guide to call out "hot" or "cold" as we try to find our way through the obstacles life presents us. I think that life does give us this kind of guidance, but most often we refuse to listen to the advice.

You know when things warm your heart and tell you to go in a particular direction. Yes, you can overdo the passion and get over-heated, but that is a signal that you need to step back from the fire. When you are feeling a chilly response from another person, it is a signal that you should not pursue this direction. If you push it, you will experience and suffer the consequences of the exposure, frostbite.

Soulution of the Day

*Pay attention to hot and cold signals,
and use your temperature to guide you through life.*

BLUNDERS

Everyone spills his milk sometime.

— EMILY POST (QUOTING A SIX-YEAR-OLD)

MAKE USE OF THE BLUNDERS to lighten up your life. When you make a blunder while introducing someone, or he or she does introducing you, laugh at it. "Tonight our guest speaker is Dr. Bernie Siegel. The rest of the program is entertainment." I loved that blunder, and it was easy to get up and be connected to the audience after that.

Emily Post once said she was waving her arms while speaking to the person sitting next to her at a formal dinner. In doing so, she knocked the dish out of the hands of the waiter as he was placing it on the table and it spilled all over the white tablecloth. The person in charge of the dinner got up and announced to everyone what had happened and asked for them to applaud her. It only improved the evening.

When we commit a blunder like showing up for an appointment or a party on the wrong day, we need to laugh about it. If you blame others for the blunder, it will make a lot of people unhappy, but laughing at the same event cheers everybody up. What I remember most about our wedding are the funny blunders and not the serious parts that went as expected.

Soulution of the Day

Enjoy the wonderful blunders we all make that keep us human.

HARD WORK

Hard work never killed anybody,
but why take a chance?

— EDGAR BERGEN

HARD WORK IS WORK you don't want to do. It is not about the physical effort you must make, but the emotional cost of the effort. When you wish you were somewhere else, doing something else, then you are doing hard work. The easiest way to know when work is too hard is to be aware of how it depletes your body and how slowly the time passes. If you continue to do hard work day after day, your body will eventually give you a day or more off, by breaking down and making it impossible for you to work at all.

Being hard at work is not the same thing. When you are immersed in your work you may be hard at work but the effect on your body is different. You may become tired but not depleted.

Yet when we are hard at work creating something, time flies and the body feels no fatigue until the work is done.

Soulution of the Day

You have the power to make choices even when it seems there are none.
If you are doing too much hard work, stop, take a break, get help, say no.

MOON LANDING

Men have become the tools of their tools.

— HENRY DAVID THOREAU

THINK OF THE AMOUNT OF MONEY spent going to the moon and into outer space. It's an interesting journey, and some of the technology involved I am sure has helped improve things on earth. But what if we had spent all the money on going within the human body, not into outer space, but inner space?

Think of the benefits to humankind that could come from genetic treatments of diseases instead of the search-and-destroy approach and all its side effects. Think about the changes we could make in various treatments of congenital defects or growing new organs to replace or eliminate diseases. A salamander is smart enough to regrow a new limb; why can't we?

We all start out as one cell that is smart enough to do all that needs to be done to create a living, breathing human being. Why don't we invest the time and money to learn how to communicate with our cells and bring back that wisdom? Then perhaps we could repair what needs to be cared for when afflictions or accidents occur. Landing on the moon is never going to provide us with the benefits that going inside the human body will.

Soulution of the Day

Before heading for the moon, we need to thoroughly know ourselves.

PRESCRIPTION #261

THE ANGELIC ITS

Angels can fly because
they take themselves lightly.

— G. K. CHESTERTON

I HAVE COME CLOSE to accidental death twice. Once when I was four years old I almost choked to death on the parts of a toy I had put in my mouth, and the other time was from a fall from a ladder. In both instances I had a sense that someone or something had intervened to save me.

I announced one night during a lecture that I must have a guardian angel. After the lecture a man came up to me and said, "You do have an angel, and I know his name." When I asked him what it was, he said, "What did you say when the ladder broke?" I told him I said, "Oh, shit." He said, "That's your angel's name."

I laughed about his explanation but since then I have begun to wonder. I was lost in traffic in Boston the other day and couldn't find the entrance to the parkway. I was very frustrated and said, "Oh, shit." At the next corner I saw the entrance I was looking for under a hospital building with no signs directing me to it. I laughed to myself, but since then I have been quite amazed at how often the situation I am in is resolved when I call out, "Oh, shit." I also have come to realize that other people have begun to have the same experience when they follow my example.

I came to the conclusion that there is a family of angels with the last name It. One of their first names must be Ohsh.

Soulution of the Day

Try calling out to the angelic "It" family the next time you need help!

MEMORIES

Memory is the cabinet of the imagination,
the treasury of reason, the registry of
conscience, and the council
chamber of thought.

— SAINT BASIL

WE ALL HAVE HAD THE EXPERIENCE OF forgetting someone's name and then five minutes later remembering it. How do we recall it? What goes on in our brains? I could ask the same question when an organ recipient receives memories from his or her new organ. What is happening to allow them to recall the information? Perhaps it is not about nerves but other forms of energy communication.

Memory is stored throughout our body. We are hearing more stories from transplant recipients about the information they receive regarding the lives of their organ donors. And memory may not be limited to our bodies. Certain types of clairvoyant healers seem to be able to read our memories by the energy state of our body parts.

We know we have access to memory, but now we need to learn the system that is present for retrieving and communicating the information. How do memories present themselves to our conscious mind even when we do not ask for the information? Who or what decides what we think about, and when? That is an interesting question that will probably never be answered by me or you.

Soulution of the Day

We all need to remain open-minded to the ways in which
we retrieve information from our minds and bodies.

WHINE OR WINE

*We are free up to the point of choice
and then the choice controls the chooser.*

— MARY CROWLEY

I JUST EMAILED A FRIEND about the fact that she complains all the time, be it about weather or her finances, and I wrote "whine, whine, whine." Then my multiple personality jumped in and suggested that instead she "wine, wine, wine." She laughed when she read it, but there is a lot of wisdom in this message too.

Do you spend your life whining about what has happened, is happening, or will happen to you? Or do you take a moment to stop and, as our son said in reaction to my play on words, "Take time to wine and dine yourself." I am not advising you to bury your troubles by consuming alcohol. I am trying to get you to see that whining while dining cures nothing, but stopping to wine and dine yourself can.

When we take the time to care for ourselves, and to serve ourselves as well as others, life changes. To give yourself time is the key. To sit back and as the lyrics tell us, "To sip a little glass of wine and look into your eyes divine," is what I am getting at and is what makes life meaningful. Take time to sit back and see the beauty of life, and don't drown it in whine.

Soulution of the Day

*The brand of whine or wine, the variety,
taste, and the year you choose, are up to you.*

NEW FRIENDS

There you sit, been side by side
for two hours, and not one of you spoke
to the fellow in the next seat.

— HARRY LAUDER

I AM TIRED OF TRAVELING, but not of the people I meet when I travel. When sitting in airports or on planes, I love to be a little different, get conversations going, and to make new friends. My friend Patch Adams says he occasionally carries some fake dog poop to the airport with him. Before his plane takes off, he drops it on the ground near his seat. He makes some pretty interesting new friends that way!

Patch and I made many friends once just walking through an airport. He is way over six feet tall and was wearing his crazy clown outfit. I am less than six feet tall and have a shaved head. Years ago when neither of us was known very well, we went to the airport after attending a meeting. My wife dropped back so she wouldn't be seen with the two escapees from a mental institution. Actually, she did it to enjoy watching the reaction of everyone in the airport we walked past. The two of us made many friends with those who had the courage to approach us.

I always go up to the purple-haired, tattooed, bizarrely dressed people and ask, "Why are you trying to be inconspicuous?" They always laugh and once they realize I am like them, we hit it off and I have a new friend.

Soulution of the Day

What are some creative things you could do
to make some interesting new friends?

PRESCRIPTION #265

INSIGHT

*Wisdom unfiltered through personal
experience does not become
a part of the moral tissue.*

— EDITH WHARTON

WHAT IS USUALLY CALLED "wisdom" is passed on generation after generation within a family because of the beneficial effect it has had over the years. However, what many of us call wisdom is really insight. Insight is a source of wisdom when it does not come from fear.

Learn not to be afraid of life and not to listen to the negative insights that come from a fear of life and not the experience of it. I love what Mark Twain said about experience: "We should be careful to get out of an experience only the wisdom that is in it — and stop there; lest we be like the cat that sits down on the hot stove-lid. She will never sit down on a hot stove-lid again — and that is well; but also she will never sit down on a cold one anymore."

So learn from the insights you obtain and those of the wise who have preceded you, so as not to live like the cat that Twain talks about. If you have been raised by a mother cat that didn't teach you this, then go out and learn the truth for yourself.

Soulution of the Day

*Those who keep themselves and their minds focused
on what is good, positive, true, and solid will gain wisdom.*

SYMPATHY

*There is nothing sweeter
than to be sympathized with.*

— GEORGE SANTAYANA

SYMPATHY IS NOT ABOUT feeling pity for the person who has experienced a significant loss or problem. Being "simpatico" is about being congenial, winsome, and pleasant. To be sympathetic is to connect with the other person so she does not feel isolated by her problem. If you fear experiencing the other person's pain, then you will not be able to be sympathetic.

Just as sympathy is not about pity, it is not about denial either. It is about accepting and relating to the person. When you do you will experience a fuller life and a feeling of closeness with the other person. In the sharing of sympathy we learn, and so we move up, in a sense, as human beings.

Being a sympathetic person will also attract others to you. They come not to share wounds and complain, but for understanding. When we are alone in our world and questioning life, a sympathetic word or touch can change our experience and help us to survive. To be held in the arms of sympathy is a gift that creates true healing.

Soulution of the Day

*Be sympathetic in your words and actions,
you never know when you may need some sympathy yourself.*

SENIOR MOMENTS

*To be seventy years young
is sometimes more cheerful and hopeful
than to be forty years old.*

— OLIVER WENDELL HOLMES

THERE ARE BENEFITS to aging that include discounts and other privileges, but for me the greatest gift is being in the moment. When you live in the moment you have no age and it allows you to experience life differently. The difference is a gift that we all should appreciate before we grow old.

When you are older you don't have to explain everything you do that doesn't make sense to your family. After all, you are older and are having a senior moment.

When you live in the moment, you stop thinking and worrying and begin to contemplate the world around you. When you do, you begin to see a much more interesting and beautiful world. You become a teacher and wise elder for the young ones, something their younger parents cannot do.

Soulution of the Day

When you live in the moment, even your "senior moments" don't matter.

PRESCRIPTION #268

IMMORTALITY

Nothing disappears without a trace.

— WERNHER VON BRAUN

I AM CONVINCED that two things are immortal: love and conscious-ness. My love lives on in all the people I have loved and who have loved me. Think about a moment in your life when you felt loved or loving, and you will feel the change in your body. The love is still with you from that original experience.

Our consciousness, I believe, continues to exist without our body; it simply is. It is as difficult to describe why I know this to be true as it is to describe God. There are many unexplainable things, such as the blind seeing when they leave their bodies. I accept that fact too, and live in peace with it.

I know my consciousness will go on and re-enter another body at the moment of birth. Can I prove it? That depends on whether you have an open mind and are willing to accept the evidence. Whether you believe in it or not, enjoy your immortality.

Soulution of the Day

*Live eternally through your love
and know your consciousness will last forever.*

WHICH WAY

Life is like that. If you can't reach your
destination by one road, try another.

— ELSA SCHIAPARELLI

HOW DO WE KNOW which road to take? Taking the easy path is not always the appropriate choice. The key is to have an open mind and not judge the path you end up on as right or wrong, but to wait to see where it takes you. Also, never admit defeat but look at other ways of getting to the point you hope to reach. When you keep your mind open, things can happen that were not planned but that end up being to your benefit. You may find that what you thought was the wrong place introduces you to things and people that make it the right place.

Do not fear deviating from the normal way and being open to unusual paths. If you go a certain way because of what others recommend, you may find yourself on the wrong path. Do not let others tell you where to go and how to get there. Follow your own path.

Soulution of the Day

No matter which way you choose to go,
ultimately it will always be the right way.

GROSS NATIONAL HAPPINESS

*I know of no more encouraging fact
than the unquestionable ability of man to
elevate his life by a conscious endeavor.*

— HENRY DAVID THOREAU

I HAVE WRITTEN ABOUT the meaning of the word *gross* and our country's Gross National Product, but I have never written about Gross National Happiness.

Then I watched *60 Minutes*. The program discussed the policies of the government of Bhutan, which is seeking a policy of Gross National Happiness. They want their citizens to be provided with the necessities essential for their happiness, such as clean water, adequate nourishment, and an education. They are controlling tourism and trying to present TV programs that will give their children more than our satellite broadcasts do.

Whether they will succeed or not remains a question, but it is a joy just to hear that their interest is in happiness, and not about being bigger, better, and richer than anyone else.

Soulution of the Day

What is required for happiness?
Maybe we all need to think that answer out again.

LISTEN
TO THE SOUNDS

Deafness is darker by far than blindness.

— HELEN KELLER

WE HEAR A GREAT DEAL, but do we listen to what we hear? For me hearing is not about the sound waves in my environment being sensed by my acoustic nerve. No matter where I am I hear things, but they are not always coming from the sounds being made around me.

I sat in the airport the other day and truly listened. I was amazed at the difference it created in me. It was more like a meditation because I heard life going on around me and not just the noise. It became a part of me and my life, and not an intrusion.

I think I understand the sounds of silence now. It is not about being deaf to the sounds of life, or the absence of sound, but the ability to hear and listen to life going on around us and in us.

Soulution of the Day

Take some time today to listen to sounds of silence.

WHAT IS WILD

In wildness is the preservation of the world.
— HENRY DAVID THOREAU

WHEN I WALK IN NATURE I realize how beautiful and orderly it is. Though it seems so simple, I know how complex it really is and how innumerable relationships, including the death of some things, are required for its survival. I think it is a misnomer to call the beauty, form, and intelligence of nature "the wilderness." It seems to me we are the wild ones, lost in the wilderness of our attempt at creation.

Our lives and cities seem far wilder and disordered in their nature and behavior than the untouched wilderness. The truth is that it is not untouched. It is touched by the hand of God, and we fail to see the beauty and order in it and go on tearing it down to replace it with our so-called civilization.

The wilderness is not wild, and civilization is not civilized. We need to return to the wholeness of nature and walk once again side by side with it. That is where the real peace and order exist that must be brought back into our lives if we are ever to be truly civilized.

Soulution of the Day

Spend some time in nature getting in sync with your true nature.

PRESCRIPTION #273

WOUNDED HEALER

*Your pain is the breaking of the shell
that encloses your understanding.
It is the bitter potion by which
the physician in you heals your sick self.*

— KAHLIL GIBRAN

I HAVE MY OWN WOUNDS, and I also learn from those who are wounded; they are my teachers. They have been to the places where others fear to go.

Some physicians have been very critical of me, and of my work, until they or their loved ones became seriously ill. Then I became a valuable asset in their desire to heal. Our wounds open us to the experience of illness and pain. We become natives and are no longer tourists in a strange land. Then we are able to join the afflicted on their journey. I am not afraid to go into their dark rooms and lives or into the dark corners of their minds to help them find the light. I too have been in the darkness and have learned to find the light.

We are all wounded, and from our wounds our power is derived. To be broken on the wheel of living is to find the secret of true healing. To live in fear is to deny yourself the ability to heal and become a healer.

Soulution of the Day

*Do not fear physical illness.
Sometimes it is the greatest of teachers.*

SERENITY

*I found serenity when I
stopped judging others.*

— MISS EMILY AND CLARENCE W. HALL

IT IS FAR EASIER to be critical of our family members and neighbors than of ourselves. When we continually judge others we do not have to look at our own weaknesses, and we have an explanation for everything that goes wrong. One of our sons, Jonathan, as a child had an invisible friend, Michael. Whenever Jon did something we were critical of, he would say, "Michael did it." He is an attorney today. We should have known.

You look out the window at your neighbor's dirty clothes hanging on the line. Then you realize it is your windows that are streaked, and when you clean them the neighbor's clothes improve dramatically. If you look through the window of blame you will never find peace.

Before you make a judgment, learn the facts and circumstances accurately. The knowledge you gain may change your opinion. Look for people's graces and not their faults, and let God do the judging. Give that a try, and you will find serenity.

Soulution of the Day

Let go of blame and see how much more serene your life becomes.

CAN YOU LISTEN?

*That is why in training our salesclerks
we stress, "Listen before you act."*

— JOHN McGRATH

I HAVE A QUOTE FROM AN ANONYMOUS SOURCE that says, "Communication begins when I understand what you thought you said." Listening is a skill that few have developed. We get bored, let our minds wander, think about what we will answer, stop talking on the phone to answer the call on the other line. We are not listening.

We are into our own thing and our own world. Until you lose your ability to hear, you don't realize what you are not listening to. Try plugging your ears for a day, and it will turn you into a better listener. I am not asking you to listen to nonsense, but I am asking you to listen and not judge so that you can truly listen. You don't have to agree with what is said to listen well.

A good listener participates and concentrates on what is being said. He or she doesn't formulate an answer and stop listening while the person is still speaking. When you listen intelligently, people tell you more. We are all storytellers and need to listen to each other's stories.

Soulution of the Day

*Make a point of improving your listening skills
so that you can become an "inspired listener."*

TOO HEAVY

*Take a deep breath, count to ten,
and tackle each task one step at a time.*

— LINDA SHALAWAY

WHAT DO YOU DO when you are asked to carry a stone that is too heavy for you to lift? What do you do when the problems confronting you seem overwhelming? You can carry the stone by breaking it into pieces first, and you can do the same thing with your problems. Do not be overwhelmed; start working on one small piece, and you will find the solution.

Break down your overwhelming tasks and problems that seem too heavy to bear. Tackle each piece, one by one, day by day, until what once seemed overwhelming is handled and completed. Then you will have a sense of accomplishment and realize just how much you can carry.

Soulution of the Day

*When something feels heavy, break it down
until one piece of it is light enough to handle. Begin there.*

JUST BEING

There is no way to peace;
peace is the way.

— A. J. MUSTE

HOW MANY OF YOU have become frantic waiting for a ride to the airport or some other event that you couldn't be late for? You get agitated and frustrated and feel helpless, yet what does this accomplish?

A Buddhist man was staying in an apartment with friends. When he was ready to leave, he went down to the street to wait for his ride to the airport. Some time later when his friends looked out the window, he was still there. His ride was obviously late, but what struck the people looking down at him was that "he wasn't waiting, he wasn't coming, he wasn't going — he was at peace, just being."

It took me a while to cultivate that state of being. But months later, when we were being driven through the mountains of Colorado to the Denver airport and had a flat tire, I was prepared. When I couldn't find the jack and the driver said her husband had it in their other car, I was still prepared. When a truck stopped and offered to help us and changed the tire faster than I could have with the proper equipment, I was ready.

Soulution of the Day

Learn to accept the spiritual flat tires in life
that redirect you to the Creator's schedule.

DIE LAUGHING

Humor is an affirmation of man's dignity, a declaration of man's superiority to all that befalls him.

— ROMAIN CARY

HOW CAN YOU DIE LAUGHING? When you are ready to go and your family is sitting around you, what will they talk about to lift your spirits? Will they have funny stories to tell about your life?

Now, if they don't remember any, you are in trouble. My father died laughing because of the many stories my mom told him about their early dates. One tale was that because he lost a coin toss, he had to take her out.

If you don't think your family has material, then get busy and build up a catalog of crazy events that they can't help recalling. My list of funny things includes a vast number, including being stopped by our town police as a suspicious character running away with full bags in my hands. The police call was related to my collecting recyclables while I was jogging. A neighbor was certain I was a thief running away from her home. It made the police laugh after they surrounded me on the road and scared the wits out of me. Other incidents relate to my crazy antics when we are out eating or shopping. When I die my family will remember all of these and laugh too.

Soulution of the Day

Start creating stories and memories funny enough for your family to tell at your bedside.

LET'S GO
FOR A WHIM

*If adults could be more like children
and allow themselves to play and indulge
a whim more often, the world would be
run by happier people.*

— ANDY MARIKA

HOW OFTEN DO YOU FOLLOW UP on an urge to do something creative or enjoyable? Do you ever get a creative idea for your home or at work but feel afraid to act on it because someone might be critical of you and your idea? If so, it's time to say, "Who cares what they think?" If you feel the urge to do something, do it.

Why restrict yourself to serious thoughts and activities? Let the child in you indulge its whims and moods. Do things that in your view improve the world or that just give you a moment of joy. What may seem like work to others can be time joyfully spent by you.

When a child gets involved in a fun activity that you don't feel is educational or meaningful, as long as it's not harmful, let her be. Or better yet, join her and learn what it feels like to just involve yourself in your emotions and desires. Never say that an activity that feels good doesn't make sense. It makes a lot of sense to do what feels good.

Soulution of the Day

*Every week indulge your whims. It will improve your life.
Learn to grow down, not up.*

PRESCRIPTION #280

PRISON OR PLAYGROUND?

*Not a shred of evidence exists
in favor of the idea that life is serious.*

— BRENDAN GILL

THE SONG SAYS life is just a bowl of cherries. We are all serving a life sentence and so, as the lyrics tell us, if life is a bowl of cherries why not enjoy the fruit rather than live in the pits? Why not find a way to make the time served a gift to yourself and humanity?

One can play while in prison; there are no rules against enjoying the confinement. Childlike humor and living in the moment lead one to a joyful life. Just as important is the way you choose to view your circumstances.

One blind ninety-year-old woman entered a nursing home when her husband died. As she was wheeled in she said, "What a beautiful place." The staff said, "You just arrived and can't see. How can you say that?" She answered, "I have a choice about what I see, and I choose to see beauty." We can view our life that way too.

The other ingredient you'll need is faith. It gives you something steadfast to hold on to. With faith you can face anything. Faith, humor, and a positive vision will help you survive the confinement of life and complete your full life sentence.

Soulution of the Day

*Your birth may be an uncontrollable event, but you do have the ability
to determine how you spend your life. You are the only one
who can serve your sentence and determine whether
your life will be spent in a prison or a playground.*

QUANTITY AND QUALITY

It's choice — not chance —
that determines your destiny.

— JEAN NIDETCH

QUANTUM PHYSICS awakened me to the nature of life and the true relationship between quantity and quality. One normally thinks of a quality product, like a fine automobile, as being desired by many and therefore as being produced in quantity. The number sold, in this case, depends on its quality.

Many of us spend our lives accumulating dollars and objects to impress others with all we possess. But what does this do to or for us as human beings? Ninety-five percent of lottery winners will tell you, five years after winning, that it ruined their life. Quantity is not the solution to life's problems.

Now enter the world of quantum physics and watch what happens when I add an electron to an existing atom. By changing the quantity of the atom, I change the quality as well.

And so it is with human beings. When we increase or alter the quantity of meaningful information, beliefs, and activities in our life, rather than the objects, we change the quality of our life for the better.

Soulution of the Day

Unlike the atom being altered by a scientist we have a choice
what to add to our personal universe. Choose wisely.

RELATE

The person who tries to live alone will not
succeed as a human being. His heart withers
if it does not answer another heart.
His mind shrinks away if he hears only
the echoes of his own thoughts and finds
no other inspiration.

— PEARL S. BUCK

LIFE IS ABOUT RELATIONSHIPS. If living life alone weren't boring, we wouldn't be here. Think about this; you are the Creator sitting around all alone on a lovely day, and another one, and another one, into infinity. One day you get up and think, "This is boring, day after day." So you create other living things to relate to and differentiate yourself from. Now you know who you are.

How you relate with others determines a great deal about the quality of your life. Studies show that people with strong spiritual connections and relationships to other living things, from plants to people, live longer, healthier lives. A recent study of elderly people showed that those who gave to others in their later years lived longer.

So give yourself a long, healthy life by giving to others and developing healing relationships. Yes, you will experience loss too, but the loss is offset by the gain. You will be sustained by the remaining relationships and carry the memories of the others with you forever, just as the Creator does, who no longer has time to be bored or lonely.

Soulution of the Day

Relate to your life. Relate to other people. Relate to all living things.

ELEPHANT

Three blind men touch an elephant. The first blind man was holding the elephant's leg and said, "I think an elephant is like the trunk of a tree." The second blind man was holding the elephant's trunk and said, "An elephant is like a large snake." The third blind man said, "An elephant is like a great wall," while touching the elephant's side.

— INDIAN PARABLE

YOU ALL KNOW THE STORY about the elephant that walked into an area where many blind men were living. They all wanted to know what the elephant was like. So when the elephant was captured, they were allowed to touch it. Of course their descriptions varied depending on the part of it they touched.

That story teaches us that until you have the complete picture you do not know what is going on and that it is best not to react based on your limited knowledge. If all the blind men had gotten together, they might have been able to come up with the truth rather than only their individual impressions.

If due to circumstances you do not have all the facts and are not able to see the whole picture, give yourself more time. Then you can accumulate the knowledge you need so your reaction will be appropriate to the circumstances as they truly exist.

Soulution of the Day

*Be slow to think you have seen the whole picture
until you are sure you have touched the whole elephant.*

TIME

Life is precious and time is a key element.
Let's make every moment count.

— HARMON KILLEBREW

TIME IS THE ONLY THING WE HAVE, and it is everything, so why do we waste it? Living in a body means we are living in time. If we are to accomplish anything with these bodies we are gifted with, we must use our time wisely.

My friend the late author and anthropologist Ashley Montagu said something that has always stayed with me. He said, "If you're ever going to die, do it at a faculty meeting. No one will notice the transition." If a good portion of your life is spent in that state of suspended animation, then get out and get going. It is no fun to live among the living dead.

Soulution of the Day

Combine good sense with your passions.
Remember that time is a precious commodity.

PRESCRIPTION #285

SILENCE

*All this talk and turmoil and noise and
movement and desire is outside of the veil;
within the veil is silence and calm and rest.*

— BAYAZID AL-RISTAMI

Fax, phones, mail, life,
Whose home is this?
What do they all want?
Where is the Silence?
I remember hearing nothing
Surrounded by sand dunes and nature.
God, how beautiful and deafening is silence,
It drowns out the fax, phones, and mail.
Silence is so loud,
Nothing can or need be heard.
I need to be silent on the inside,
Until I can return to the silence outside.

Soulution of the Day

When the noise in your life gets too loud,
listen to the silence within. But of course if you can escape
to the ocean, that will help too.

WIZARD OF OZ

*We are at our best when the doctor
who resides within each patient
has the chance to go to work.*

— ALBERT SCHWEITZER

EACH OF US HAS A WIZARD OF OZ within us. Sometimes I think it is a Wizard of Odd, but no matter which, this wizard can do amazing things. For instance, you are part of a study for a new treatment for cancer, taking laetrile. Your tumor disappears and you feel fine until the report of the study says that laetrile is of no value. Your tumor returns. Your doctor says she has new and refined laetrile and explains that the study failed because it wasn't refined properly. You are treated, and the tumor disappears again. Then a final negative report on the study appears, and you die a few days later.

Placebos can stop hair from falling out almost as well as the drugs currently on the market. They can stop bleeding, pain, nausea and vomiting, and more. One of my patients was nauseated and asked her daughter to get her Compazine from the drawer. Her daughter handed her a pill, and she took it and was well within minutes. That evening she and the daughter realized that instead of Compazine she had received Coumadin, an anticoagulant, because her daughter had seen the letter *C* on the pill and assumed it was the right one.

Doctors rub children's skin with an alcohol pad before needle punctures. I always told the children it would numb their skin. One-third had no pain, another third said it didn't work well, and the others said, ouch, it didn't work at all. The treatment that cures you may not be what really cures you; it may be your belief in it, and the Wizard of Oz that resides in each of us.

Soulution of the Day

Call upon the Wizard whenever you need to heal.

THE
WEAKER SEX?

*Most men act so tough and strong
on the outside because on the inside,
we are scared, weak, and fragile.
Men, not women, are the weaker sex.*

— JERRY RUBIN

WOMEN ARE OFTEN CALLED the weaker sex, but there is no question that feminine qualities are survivor qualities. This fact is substantiated by statistics.

Innumerable studies show us the many different qualities of men and women. Women are comfortable talking and exploring feelings. Men are always trying to fix things and get frustrated when the problem is unfixable on a mental or physical level. Sometimes when they do not want to deal with an issue directly, they withdraw or disappear.

I know a woman whose husband never offered her any help at home. He went to work every day at the office and then would come home and refuse to be of help to her. Even when she asked, he found excuses. After many years of this, she just went about her work without asking anymore.

When he died, she was finally able to get him to help. She had him cremated and his ashes put into a kitchen timer. Now he helps her out when she is cooking dinner for herself and her guests.

Soulution of the Day

There are always options when you have an open mind.

SEASONS

Spring passes and one remembers one's innocence
Summer passes and one remembers one's exuberance
Autumn passes and one remembers one's reverence
Winter passes and one remembers one's perseverance.

— YOKO ONO

EVERY SEASON has its own gifts and effects on us. In the winter people hibernate and most do not dream, even when they are sleeping. After the winter holidays the obituary page is full. You will notice that when spring arrives the page is not so crowded with faces and names. But during this cold season, people sit in the dark and lose their will to live instead of using the time to meditate, dream, listen, read, learn, or create. They are not like the seed preparing itself for the spring, when it will burst forth with new life and energy to bask in the warmth of the sun.

The spring sunlight awakens and calls to us to come out of our darkness and depression. It calls us forth, and our spirit is rekindled. Springtime awakens the survivor in all of us. We step out into the light and feel the warmth of the sun on our skin and are stimulated to actively participate in life again, to bloom and seek what sustains us. Everywhere we look we are stimulated by new life and color and cannot resist nature's call to live.

The summer sun brings out our playfulness. It is a time for vacation and rest. The fall reminds us with its brilliant colors to enjoy the light while we still have it, to expose our unique color and nature, and prepare for the dark times ahead. Each season offers its own lessons and blessings.

Soulution of the Day

Use the seasons for the reasons they were created.
Be ready to bloom and blossom.

PRESCRIPTION #289

AMERICA

Men become what they are,
sons of God, by becoming what they are,
brothers of their brothers.

— MARTIN BUBER

THE PREAMBLE to the Declaration of Independence says, "We hold these truths to be self-evident; that all men are created equal; that they are endowed by their creator with certain unalienable rights; that among these are life, liberty and the pursuit of happiness."

But are we all equal? My ancestors came to this country to escape persecution and save their lives. There are Americans whose ancestors were brought here as slaves to be persecuted. There is no one American experience, even if our declarations and laws speak of equal treatment. As long as people do not see themselves and each other as members of one family, there is no equality.

When you consider how many countries there are in the world, and that each has many minority groups within it, you can see the trouble we are in and headed for. Until we become one planet under God, or not under God, whatever makes everyone happy, with liberty and justice for all, we are nothing.

I speak all over America and outside it too, and I see the differences among people. But I can always find common themes to talk about because we all are suffering from the same affliction — life. When life becomes a family problem, I will be proud to say I am an American and a citizen of the world.

Soulution of the Day

Be a lover and a member of the family of humankind
and list your nationality last.

HELP ME TO LIVE

*I can't take you home with me so I need to
know how to live between office visits.*

— A PATIENT

IT IS SAD HOW UNPREPARED for life we are. About eight hundred
years ago the Jewish philosopher and physician Maimonides wrote
A Guide for the Perplexed. Things haven't changed much; we still
need a book entitled *A Traveler's Guide to Life.*

To guide my patients through difficult times, I began support
groups to help them to live between office visits. Helping them to
live means getting them to realize they have permission to live their
life, to move, change jobs, live by the seashore or the mountains, put
their oldest jeans on, and just do what feels right. What I discovered, of course, was what everyone knows but what doctors are not
taught. If you help people to really live, it is good for their health,
and many don't die when they are "supposed" to.

We don't need help living in a physical sense. Our body knows
how to do that. It doesn't need instructions; it needs the right
messages. We need help learning how to live aware of our feelings.
There is no reason to be perplexed. If you can feel, you can heal
your life, and perhaps cure your body as a side effect.

Soulution of the Day

Always be open to help, both giving and receiving it.

AWARD CEREMONY

*Glory follows virtue
as if it were its shadow.*

— CICERO

THERE ARE SO MANY CEREMONIES at which people are presented honors for things I question. So many awards seem to have no meaning or are very shallow. What we need is an award that is given out to outstanding human beings.

My friend Ashley Montagu certainly agreed. He said, "At graduations, many honorary degrees are given to horses' asses." He hoped some day that "they will give a degree to an entire horse."

Why do we admire what is superficial and related to material things? We should respect and honor people for things like wisdom, compassion, charity, love, and faith. And do it often. We do have some awards for noble deeds, but far more frequently, and almost always on prime-time TV, we see the meaningless awards that are forgotten in two weeks.

Let us hope that someday we will have a "full horse" award. It would be like the Oscars, but far more meaningful.

Soulution of the Day

Live each day in order to win the "full horse" award.

PARADE OF LIFE

Forget past mistakes. Forget failures.
Forget everything except what you are
going to do now and do it.

— WILLIAM DURANT

LIFE IS A PARADE. Sometimes we march along and realize we have passed by what we were looking for. What do we do? Stand there and drop out of the parade? March on with regrets? Feel bad about how we looked or that everything we wanted was on the wrong side of the street? It's past! Forget it and march on!

Sometimes our parade isn't so pretty, and the crowd isn't interested in us. If we drag everything we have passed with us, we will destroy the present. We have no future when we live in the past.

We even talk about past lives. Whether you believe in them or not, the same principle applies. If you are living a past life, you are destroying your present one. In therapy people come to understand why they are acting the way they are and how the past is affecting them. They learn to let go, move on, and not sit in the same class-room year after year. They graduate and commence a new life.

Soulution of the Day

The past is over unless you rebirth it every day.

DAILY DOSE

We have forgotten the age-old fact
that God speaks chiefly through
dreams and visions.

— C. G. JUNG

WHAT WE REQUIRE IN DAILY DOSES to stay well is a story a day and a dream each night. When we are ready to see what our day's teaching tale is about and recall our night's dream, we grow and learn from our finest teacher, the Inner Self.

Through our dreams and daily stories, our Inner Self speaks to us. When we pay attention to these stories and dreams, our minds are better able to process our exhaust fumes. The exhaust within us stays toxic until we allow it into our conscious awareness so that it can be recycled and released. These stories and dreams protect our true selves and when taken in a daily dose, they heal us.

Soulution of the Day

Daily reflection on your stories and dreams
will help keep the doctor away.

TARGET PRACTICE

*You got to be careful
if you don't know where you're going,
because you might not get there.*

— YOGI BERRA

YOUR TARGET IN LIFE helps you to direct your course. So before you aim, be sure you choose the right target.

What are you aiming for? What is your goal? What goals are you trying to achieve? What are you trying to hit? These are the questions you need to ask yourself, because they tell you your direction and where you will end up.

The more target practice you engage in, the more likely you are to hit the bull's-eye.

Soulution of the Day

*Take the time to refocus on your target.
Ask the questions often to be sure to hone in on your center.*

OMNIPOTENT OR IMPOTENT?

The belief in a non-omnipotent God is less depressing than the belief that the destinies of the universe are at the mercy of a being who, with the resources of omnipotence at his disposal, decided to make a universe no better than this.

— JOHN M. E. M'TAGGART

I DO NOT BELIEVE that the chaotic aspects of existence prove or disprove anything about a God. In order for living things to survive, they have to be prepared for change. If your heart couldn't change its beat, you might die under stressful conditions. So too with the weather; if it never rained and was always sunny, could we survive? We may ask, Who needs tornadoes or earthquakes? But it may be because of them that we are capable of surviving other events too.

I do not believe that any one individual has worked this all out, but I do believe there is an intelligence, energy, and consciousness behind everything, or we wouldn't be here. If you ask astronomers about the chance of all this happening and our surviving accidentally, they'll say it is no accident.

So perhaps our God is neither omnipotent nor impotent, but just a good general contractor who has built into the structure the ability to survive chaotic events. If we were only prepared for the same environment day after day, any change would destroy us.

Soulution of the Day

No matter what you believe, you must embrace change as a part of God's plan.

PERFECTION

The bottom line is that (a) people are never perfect, but love can be, (b) that is the one and only way that the mediocre and vile can be transformed, and (c) doing that makes it that. We waste time looking for the perfect lover, instead of creating the perfect love.

— TOM ROBBINS

I SPENT MY LIFE looking for the perfect woman, and when I found her I proposed marriage to her. She looked at me and said, "Thank you for the compliment, but I cannot accept your proposal because I am looking for the perfect man."

What every woman wants isn't really the perfect man, though she does want someone reasonable. What she truly wants is a life of her own that is respected. The man who is willing to give her that gift is in essence the perfect man, even with all his imperfections.

Most of us give up our lives to please our parents, teachers, spouses, families, bosses, and more. Instead I say, "Stop losing your life and find it where you know it exists; within your heart's desire." You can't ever be a perfect man or woman if you do not become yourself. Perfection is about self-identity and not the absence of faults.

Soulution of the Day

Become your perfect self, problems and all.

HOLD ON

Let an Angel hold your hand.

— TERYL SEAMAN

I WAS HAVING A VERY DIFFICULT DAY as a surgeon, with many emergencies and difficult patients. I had no time to eat and was starved and exhausted. Finally I had a few quiet moments, late in the afternoon, and opened my special lunch box. This lunch box is red, with the word *love* written all over it in white letters. Bobbie fixes my lunch and puts it in the box every morning.

By having it with me I know I will at some time be able to eat, no matter what my day is like.

That day I opened it, and taped in the cover was a note: "Hold on. We love you." I felt so lucky to have an intuitive wife who knew I was going to have a difficult day and sent me that note. I held on, and when I got home thanked her for her therapeutic note.

"What therapeutic note?" she said.

I replied, "The 'hold on' note in my lunch. I held on and got through the day."

She smiled and said, "Honey, it was a big sandwich with a lot of vegetables. I just wanted you to hold onto it!"

Since then my wife sends her love with lunch and a note that says, "This is a two-hand sandwich." It's still very therapeutic!

Soulution of the Day

Sometimes things appear just at the right moment to help us hold on.

UGLY DUCKLING

*To be born in a duck's nest, in a farmyard,
is of no consequence to a bird, if it is
hatched from a swan's egg.*

— HANS CHRISTIAN ANDERSEN

FOR HEALTH REASONS, my mother was not supposed to risk a pregnancy. She did, however, and when her labor started it continued for days. She was considered too great a risk for a cesarean section. So the doctor reached up into the uterus with forceps, and pulled me out. My mother said, "I wasn't handed a baby, I was handed a purple melon."

My mother went on to say that they took the melon home, where my father wrapped my head in a kerchief so no one could see me. Then they put me in a covered carriage at the back of the house so they wouldn't upset the neighbors. I was an ugly duckling but still loved and accepted into the nest.

I also had what the ugly duckling didn't have, a grandmother. She took me, and according to my mother, poured oil over my head and face every few hours and pushed everything back where it belonged. The loving hands changed me from an ugly duckling into a swan.

Over fifty years later my shaved head was massaged with oil for the first time by a female massage therapist. Her hands took me back to my infancy. I went into a trance that frightened everyone in attendance. "You were gone. We didn't know what happened to you." I did. I went back to being a baby swan.

Soulution of the Day

Loving hearts and hands can turn even ugly ducklings into swans.

MEANING

*Whatever words we utter should be chosen
with care, for people will hear them and be
influenced by them for good or ill.*

— BUDDHA

ANTHROPOLOGIST ASHLEY MONTAGU said it well: "The meaning of a word is the action it produces." The meaning of your life is related to what you do and what you say. If what you say does not lead to an action that is consistent with what you do, then your life's message is not honest. When you speak what you do not believe, you are being dishonest to yourself and others.

We are predominately known by what we do. However, our words can be just as powerful because of the effect they have on others and what they may lead them to do.

What we say is not incidental. It can hold great meaning, particularly if we are in a position of power or influence. Knowing this, we must use our position to guide others through our actions and the actions our words produce.

Soulution of the Day

Make your life consistent in action and word.

WOMAN

Adam said to God:
"What will she cost me? An arm and a leg?
What can I get for a rib?"
And the rest is history.

— A QUIP USED BY BOBBIE SIEGEL

AS I SIT AND WRITE I realize I can only speak from my limited perspective as a male member of the species. Women have been my teachers, and I think I feel more comfortable with them than with men. This is because of all the years women were in the majority in the group therapy sessions I led.

I think our planet would be a healthier place if we gave women more say in how things are run. They are into life and survival far more than the men, and yet at times our society has made them into second-class citizens by judging them more harshly, not letting them vote, paying them less, and even making them pay for birth control pills while drug therapy for male erectile problems is covered by medical insurance.

It is time to right this wrong and for all to become aware of the value of woman.

Soulution of the Day

I do not write this out of guilt, but respect.
Men, get behind the women and help them to have a full life too.

FALL

*Winter is an etching, spring a watercolor,
summer an oil painting, and autumn
a mosaic of them all.*

— STANLEY HOROWITZ

*The wind blows and the leaves are hurrying about.
The sun shines and nature's rainbow glows.
I am in awe of this creation.
I try to hold this moment.
There's the struggle.
Perhaps the solution is to let go
And simply cherish the now.*

Soulution of the Day

Marvel in the beauty of "tonow" and eliminate today and tomorrow.

FORTUNE COOKIES

What I found were "coincidences"
which were connected so meaningfully
that their "chance" concurrence
would be incredible.

— C. G. JUNG

THE OTHER NIGHT I needed a message to help me direct my life and picked out a fortune cookie for advice. Well, it was very helpful. It made me wonder who had sent the cookie at that moment for me to read. Is it all really chance, or is there an intelligence at work here? I reflected on such happenings and how they end up affecting our lives.

Sometimes what seems like a small or even upsetting event can end up saving your life. I used to call these events "spiritual flat tires." Even though they upset you when they happen, like the flat tire that makes you miss a plane that ends up crashing, they were ultimately there to help you. I always say there is a schedule to the universe that we all need to get on and be in harmony with.

Soulution of the Day

Look for the fortune cookies and seeming detours
that are sent to get you on track for your true destination.

PRESCRIPTION #303

SUICIDE

Guns aren't lawful; nooses give;
Gas smells awful; you might as well live.

— DOROTHY PARKER

MANY YEARS AGO a dear friend of mine told me he was very depressed and dealing with many problems. One day when his wife left the house to go shopping, he decided to commit suicide. He went to the garage to start his car and planned to sit there and inhale the exhaust, but he couldn't get the car started. So he called AAA. When the service man arrived and asked what the problem was, what could he say: "I am trying to commit suicide and the damn car won't start"?

Another friend with AIDS decided he would commit suicide and not have to face his disease. He went out to the garage and started his car with no trouble. But after an hour or two, he realized you don't die if you have a diesel; you just get filthy.

Both of these men went on living full lives. The compassion of the AAA serviceman changed my friend's life. The man sensed a problem and stayed with him until his wife came home. My friend with AIDS went back in the house, bathed, cleaned up, and decided to get a new wardrobe and redecorate his house. He found a new life and is doing fine.

Soulution of the Day

Give your life a charge, start it up, and put your foot on the accelerator.

WHO ARE THE STRANGERS?

*Fear makes strangers of people
who would be friends.*

— SHIRLEY MACLAINE

MANY YEARS AGO I arrived at Grand Central Station in New York on my way home from college. All the freshmen at Colgate were obligated to greet everyone they met on campus. The habit was so ingrained that I started saying hello to all the people I passed in the station. I soon stopped because the more I said hello, the more people backed away from me.

The other day at the airport, I walked over to a child eating an enormous pretzel and playfully asked for a bite. Most children pull away and don't want to share their treats with a stranger. But this little boy offered me a bite. I was touched by his generosity and love. I said, "No, that's okay, you finish it." He then walked over to his dad, who was looking out at departing planes, and tugged on his pant leg. When his dad looked down the boy said, "Do you have money for another pretzel?" I told his dad what had transpired and what a gift his son was.

Another time Bobbie and I were out biking and saw a neighbor's dog tied to a tree about a mile from his home. I thought he had been tied up by someone who saw him roaming with a broken leash. As I approached him he jumped up and started licking my face. I untied him and started toward his home. Just then his owner came out of the nearby dentist's office and explained she had tied him there to keep him away from the dentist's dog. She was surprised he accepted me and was going with me. I wasn't surprised at all.

Soulution of the Day

Children and animals often open themselves to those who care. Adults are the problem. We need to be like the children and animals and accept the greetings of those who offer them. Otherwise, how will we ever get to be one family?

WINTER

You can't shake hands with a clenched fist.
— **INDIRA GANDHI**

Winter is here,
The trees huddle for warmth.
Their arms intertwine
They touch each other
And become one family
Living their true nature.
Winter is here,
People's houses are dark.
Isolated, alone.
They do not reach out.
And with closed blinds,
They do not illuminate, see, or touch.
It is cold and unnatural.

Soulution of the Day

Embrace others; don't give the people in your life the
"cold shoulder." Become a luminary for those you meet on the road of life.

PRESCRIPTION #306

THE FOUR ELEMENTS

He who knows what sweets and virtues
are in the ground, the waters, the plants,
the heavens, and how to come at these
enchantments, is the rich and royal man.

— RALPH WALDO EMERSON

WIND, EARTH, FIRE, AND WATER are the four elements we all need in our lives. As a physician, my view of these elements was quite skeptical. It all seemed too simple, considering the technological advances we have made in the last century. But I now see these elements as a vital part of life.

Wind is the breath of life. In many languages the words for *breath* and *spirit* are the same. It is what God breathed into Adam's nostrils. The wind at your back or beneath your wings provides the energy to move you forward and create life.

The earth represents our food and true nourishment. We need to nourish ourselves, as do the roots that feed all growing things. Earth gives us strength and stability, a foundation on which to stand during difficult or stormy times. The earth is our Mother.

Fire illuminates the darkness. We all must strive to become luminaries and light the way for others. Fire also provides warmth and comfort but needs wind to burn. It provides the heat of passion and pressures us to change when things get too hot. Without feelings and emotions, life would be meaningless, and we would never strive to regulate the temperature of life.

Water can quench our thirst when we experience dry times. It can put out raging fires, soften the earth, and nourish living things. Even more important, it can spread life to every corner of creation and to all who drink of it.

Soulution of the Day

Each of the four elements can destroy or sustain us.
It is our challenge to balance and maintain them.

THE
WRONG TURN

Let go and let God.
— TWELVE-STEP SLOGAN

ONE DAY I MADE A WRONG TURN on the parkway. There was no sign to help, and I was too proud to ask for directions. I had to change my way and turn around. So, I took a deep breath and let God take the wheel.

Everything worked out because God has had her driver's license longer than I have. Who knows what the good Lord got me to miss by this detour...perhaps things that I am better off not colliding with! When we believe we are on the wrong road in life, we have to let God do the driving. We may have to turn around to head in the right direction, but if we are willing, we can learn from our detours.

I guess I took the right turn after all. Look what I learned when I let go and let God into the driver's seat.

Soulution of the Day

Who is at the wheel in your life?
Are you heading in the right direction?
What have you learned from life's detours?

PRESCRIPTION #308

WALK
YOUR TALK

*It is no use walking anywhere to preach
unless our walking is our preaching.*

— SAINT FRANCIS OF ASSISI

WE ALL HAVE HEARD THE SAYING about walking the walk and not just talking the talk. Yet how many of us live the message we are preaching? How many of us are willing to live the sermon? It is so much easier to deliver the sermon than it is to live the message.

For all the years I have been speaking, my wife and members of our family are almost always in the audience, and when they are not there physically, they are there in spirit. I have seen the effect it has on people to have my wife and children listening to me. They know I am being honest about what I say and do because my witnesses are right there. They love it when my wife interrupts me to make a correction, just as she would if we were sitting at home.

I do not accept the words of those who place themselves above me while acting in a way that is in conflict with their words. If they are being abusive to others and self-destructive, what they say may be true, but I want to hear it from someone who manifests the truth in their own life.

Soulution of the Day

*Align your actions with your words.
Live what you preach and be a role model.*

SECOND WIND

Only the very exceptional individuals
push to their extremes.

— WILLIAM JAMES

I HAVE RUN SEVERAL MARATHONS, and I know that at some point something happens in my body and I feel as if I were just starting the race. We all have this resource within us, but most of us never test ourselves for fear of failing. As a surgeon, when I am operating on someone, I have the energy to stand for hours without eating, drinking, or feeling tired.

I've also watched our daughter care for one of her sons, who has many medical problems. It's amazing how she maintains her strength and ability to be a loving mother through many crises.

Our bodies will respond to our needs and desires. We were created to survive. When the will to live, to finish a race or project, or to care for someone is uppermost in our desires and mind, the message gets through to our body and we get a second wind. It is as though the meaningful desires and needs call up a store of energy from within.

Soulution of the Day

When you find yourself pushed to extremes and you think
you have no more reserves, be assured that your second wind is on the way.

MOURNING

Absence and death are the same...
only that in death there is no suffering.

— WILLIAM LANDOR

WHEN SOMEONE YOU LOVE DIES it can be very painful to bury them. What you love is gone, and you are burying your beloved, never to be seen or touched again.

In the past I turned to the darkness when I lost a beloved. I would wear black and think dark thoughts about what I had lost and how empty life seemed. Time and experience have helped. I have learned how to handle loss better now than I did in the past. I have realized that the loved one was not asking me to remain in mourning to prove my love.

After my father died, my pain was turned into joy by a simple story. I knew my father would have liked it. It was about a man whose daughter died. He became depressed and unable to function until he had a dream in which he was in heaven seeing all the dead children walking by carrying bright candles. One child was holding a dark candle, and when the father went to light it, he realized the child was his daughter.

"Let me light your candle," he said.

The child replied, "It is, Father, but your tears keep putting it out."

That story helped me to return to life.

After one of our dogs died, every morning I would walk by and leave a stone on his grave. Each day I searched for a stone because my heart felt that way. Then I awakened one morning feeling as if the dog had sent me a message about seeing the beauty of the day, and not just the stones. That morning and ever since, I bring a flower. The dog's gift was to remind me to see the beauty all around and to search for the most beautiful flower to bring to his spirit.

Soulution of the Day

There is a time for everything: a time to mourn and a time to heal,
and a time to turn toward the light and the beauty.

PRESCRIPTION #311

TEACHERS

When the student is ready,
the teacher appears.

— TAOIST SAYING

THE SUFI POET RUMI SAID, "Criticism polishes my mirror." He taught me that everyone is my teacher. If you are trying to be a better human being, then look for teachers. They might be your colleagues, your family, and even your pets. My family, nurses, and patients have always been my teachers. They tell me when I could be a better doctor, father, husband, and so on.

The people who I worry about are the ones that always blame everyone else, never do their homework, and do not accept the fact that they have anything to learn or that they can ever do anything wrong.

Once a teacher has led you to understand how to improve at what you are doing and at being who you are, do your homework and ask them to continue to grade you on your progress. Life is a school, and teachers are everywhere if you are willing to attend the class called Life 101.

Soulution of the Day

See your day as a classroom and be aware of the different subjects
and teachers available to you for your further education.
Life is a great teacher.

LOOK
TO THIS DAY

*Our main business is not to see
what lies dimly at a distance, but to do
what lies clearly at hand.*

— THOMAS CARLYLE

WHEN WE SPEND OUR TIME always focused ahead it is hard to live in the moment. Yes, you can plan for tomorrow, but you don't start living it until it is *today*. How you get through life is the same way sand gets through an hourglass, grain by grain. So it is with the day and your difficulties. If you deal with what needs to be done one grain at a time, eventually your hourglass of problems will empty itself.

How would you finish the sentence "When I get _____ then I will be alright"? It is not in the "when I get" that you must live, but in the *now*. The Indian writer Kalidasa wrote, "Today well-lived makes every yesterday a dream of happiness and every tomorrow a vision of hope."

Soulution of the Day

*Shut the doors to the past and the future.
Live and look well to this day.*

BEDSCAPES

Everyone needs beauty as well as bread,
places to play in and pray in,
where nature may heal and cheer
and give strength to body and soul alike.

— JOHN MUIR

A FRIEND OF MINE, Yosaif August, has devised something called a "bedscape." It is a beautiful outdoor scene that you can hang in your hospital room. Why would you want to do that? Studies show that people who can see nature from their hospital room or have scenes of the outdoors instead of abstract paintings in their room heal faster and experience less pain.

The colors of nature are no accident, nor are the forms it takes. Tonight as I type this there is a full moon. What if the moon were a gray jagged object? It would not be very attractive to look at. Instead, we have a circle of white light, the circle being a mandala and symbol of wholeness that affects us in ways we are not always aware of.

In spring, summer, and fall, the vibrant colors bring joy and an uplifting feeling. In winter, with darkness and somber shades of gray, more people become ill and die. Is it an accident that the short, dark, cold days affect our desire to survive, while the spring brings life to all living things?

Soulution of the Day

Bring some color and images of nature
into your landscape and livingscape to heal your body and soul.

PRESCRIPTION #**314**

COURAGE

*One who puts on his armor
should not boast like one who takes it off.*

— 1 KINGS 20:11

WHEN I SEE THE WORD *courage,* first I think of warriors ready
to engage in battle knowing they are risking their lives to protect
others. But then my mind comes back to my life and the courage it
takes to just get up and face each day. Life is the battle we all must
face. Some of us seem to have a bigger burden than others, but that
relates to the inner strength of individuals and not their problems.

I've never met anyone who wants to change afflictions with
anyone else, even when they feel no one is worse off than themselves. So our only alternative is to have the courage to face the day
and live. Many choose death as a way out. They work hard at
killing their bodies as quickly as possible. I choose life even with its
pain, tears, and loss and want the opportunity to experience it all.

I have the courage to outlive loved ones and help them to go
in my arms. I open my arms as a beloved companion and fellow
warrior of life, one who has the courage to take off his armor,
provide warmth and comfort, compassion and healing. Each of
us needs to be willing to remove our armor so we can be totally
present with each other.

Soulution of the Day

*If you awakened today ready for the battle of your lifetime,
give yourself a medal of honor.*

SENSE OF HUMOR

*A sense of humor is a major defense
against minor troubles.*

— MIGNON MCLAUGHLIN

I BELIEVE THE FOUNDATION OF ONE'S LIFE should be love, but something has to hold the foundation and the structure together when the earth quakes. The only cement I know that is strong enough to do that is a healthy sense of humor. When we laugh, wounds are healed.

I believe a good sense of humor benefits all our relationships. My wife and I have learned to laugh at each other. When we laugh, our hurts and wounds are no longer felt, and we go on living.

I can think of two times when my wife spilled really hot drinks in my lap. Both times I was wearing a seat belt and couldn't escape. When she spilled hot coffee in my lap while I was driving late at night, it awakened me more than drinking it would have. So I thanked her for waking me up. On a plane, after she spilled a hot drink on me, she said she used herbal tea because she knew that caffeine wasn't good for me. Yes, we laughed, the pain stopped, and the love stood firm. I love her when she laughs and when she makes me laugh.

Having a house full of pets also helps to maintain our sense of humor. They seem to know what is important and how to get us to laugh at life by enjoying the simple things and allowing us to share the laughter with them.

Soulution of the Day

Don't overlook the power of a healthy sense of humor.

CREATIVE VISUALIZATION

Every moment of your life is infinitely creative and the universe is endlessly bountiful. Just put forth a clear enough request, and everything your heart truly desires must come to you.

— SHAKTI GAWAIN

HOW OFTEN DO WE PICTURE A GOOD LIFE? How often do we see trouble ahead and all the things we fear happening? We are more likely to create what we are visualizing, so we need to be very aware of what pictures we are focusing on.

Our bodies do not really know the difference between what we visualize and what we are actually doing. The messages it receives are based on the internal changes the body undergoes because of our visions and our actions. If we continue to visualize what we feel is wrong with us, we will remain in that image. The day we change the image of ourselves and our world, we will see a new reflection.

Use your time to visualize what you actually want to happen. Interrupt your day every few hours to visualize a positive future. Genes respond to your behavior, activities, and images, so your body will follow suit.

Creative imagery, hypnosis, and even dreaming can guide you. As mentioned in the Bible, God speaks in dreams and visions. So get in touch with the language of creation and visualize your highest good.

Soulution of the Day

Create the image that you desire for yourself and your life. Then see it, believe it, and live it.

CAREGIVERS

Anything less than a conscious commitment to the important is an unconscious commitment to the unimportant.

— STEPHEN COVEY

CAREGIVERS ARE MEMBERS OF A TEAM, but the captain of the team also needs attention and care. If the team metaphor doesn't work for you, think of yourself as a member of an orchestra. Each person plays his or her own part, which is necessary for the proper result. The conductor plays an important role as well.

My mom is ninety-four years old as I write this. I would change things if I were in charge of how and where she lives, but that is my problem. When I think about what she needs and wants, then I become her caregiver, and when I don't, I am a caretaker. The caretaker takes charge and is not just giving but directing the performance, and that is inappropriate. Caregivers are not to impose their needs on the person they are caring for.

If you are having problems being a caregiver, remember, you have needs too. So learn to say no to what you can't or do not want to do, and do what you can. Volunteers live longer, healthier lives, but it is their choice to give care. We must remember that even the caregiver needs a caregiver at times. When you need a rest, take it.

Soulution of the Day

Give your care freely out of love, and you will be rewarded.
Just include yourself on the list of recipients.

PRESCRIPTION #318

MOTHER NATURE

*Our concern is not how to worship
in the catacombs, but how to worship
in the skyscrapers.*

— ABRAHAM JOSHUA HESCHEL

TODAY I AM DISTURBED by the word *skyscraper*. I have just returned from a walk in the woods with my little dog, Furphy. I felt the sanctity of Mother Nature today in a way that touched my heart. With the trees around me I felt as if I were in a sanctuary, closer to my Creator than I could ever be in a building, be it a chapel, church, mosque, or synagogue. Such buildings are built to perform rituals in, impress people, and scrape the sky to get attention.

The trees grow tall enough to touch the sky but possess an inherent gentleness that buildings can never attain. The trees bend and sway and do not scrape Mother Nature's garments or tear at her wholeness and holiness. They survive earthquakes and tornadoes because they are rooted in nature, while the scrapers of the sky are more likely to crack and fall and need to be rebuilt.

Soulution of the Day

*When we respect nature and cease scraping the sky,
we will return to our true nature — Mother Nature.*

GATHERINGS

Expect people to be better than they are;
it helps them to become better.
But don't be disappointed when they are not;
it helps them to keep trying.

— MERRY BROWNE

OFTEN WE ARE REQUIRED to participate in gatherings. From holiday and office parties to family reunions, these can be difficult. The expectations we have before we go will color our experience when we get there.

When you expect to be loved, you behave differently. Think about going to a family affair where you expect everyone to praise and love you. Now think about going to an event where everyone will be critical of you and your behavior. Feel the difference in your body and attitude.

Go expecting to be loved, and you will be. Because of the love of my parents, wife, and family, I anticipate that people will love me. I have found myself laughing when I am invited to a meeting where I expect to be loved and am instead criticized. When my critics ask why I am laughing, I explain the problem is that I feel loved and expected them to love me too. The meeting always goes well after that.

Soulution of the Day

Always expect the best and see what happens.

TIME FOR EVERYTHING

*Come out of the circle of time
and into the circle of love.*

— RUMI

DOES TIME EXIST? Is it real? Does a tree know the time? Does the ocean? Who created time? Who said, "You're late"? Why is it one o'clock? In the Divine, there is time for everything; it is always the right time. You are never too late…and are always on time. Does light or energy concern itself with time? Everything in the universe is subject to change and everything is on schedule, or so my bumper sticker says. Love is like that; time is lost in love. Love is a trance state that heals all wounds. Love is energy, so it knows no time and no physical limitations.

Soulution of the Day

Lose track of time by showing your love for someone.

LIFEGUARDS

*Our scientific power has outrun
our spiritual power. We have guided
missiles and misguided men.*

— MARTIN LUTHER KING JR.

IT SEEMS INAPPROPRIATE that we have people sitting on the beach watching us go in the water while no one guides us as we plunge into life. We all need lifeguards. We need someone who can safely direct us to find our ability to stay afloat in the sea of life, especially when parents, teachers, and religions are not giving us the help we need.

Our children are in great danger of drowning. It is incredible that the headlines are full of news about children killing their teachers and parents. We must let the children know we are here to be their lifeguards and life guides. We need to be there when they get in over their heads or flounder in deep waters and pull them to safety. We have to keep them on shore when the sea of life is turbulent. We can't just sit by and watch them go down.

Soulution of the Day

*Please sign up for duty. Work a shift so that our children
will be guarded and guided to a safe, dry place where they can live
free of the threat of stormy seas. Be there so when the occasional
severe storm does occur they will know where to turn
to find a life preserver.*

SELF-DISCOVERY

Who in the world am I?
Ah, that is the question!

— LEWIS CARROLL

DISCOVERING WHO WE ARE is a major undertaking. Too often we destroy who we are in order to create what others want from us.

I use drawings a great deal to help people learn who they are. It may be a simple drawing of yourself or one that shows you in various careers or educational pursuits. The symbolic language from the unconscious tells the truth. There is a deeper wisdom that comes from, I have to say it, God knows where. It is the instinctive, intuitive wisdom that we so often bury or block out of our consciousness.

Life is meant to be about self-discovery and not self-destruction. The joy is in trying, experiencing, tasting, feeling, and finding ourselves.

Soulution of the Day

Do not destroy the person within you that you need
to meet, acknowledge, and become.

DANCING
AND SINGING

True health is vital energy flow.
Restricted energy flow leads to ailment.

— CHINESE MEDICINE

LIFE THRIVES ON RHYTHM. The tick of a clock, the beat of your heart, and the cadence of your walk all have an inherent rhythm. Music, dancing, and singing all affect us. When we move and sing to a beat we are stimulating our minds and bodies.

Children have no problem moving and dancing without concern for how well they are doing it. But as we grow up, we begin to sit out dances and don't sing our song. That is because we feel we are not good enough, or graceful enough, or dressed right, or whatever it is we worry about. We are always concerned about what others might see or hear and then say about us.

When you sit life out you lose touch with its rhythm, and your body loses its vitality. So sing your song, even if it's just in the shower. Dance your dance, even if it's just in your living room, and find rhythm in your life.

Soulution of the Day

Turn on the music and sing and dance your heart out.
Don't grade yourself. Participate in the dance of life.

PRESCRIPTION #324

CRITICS

It is not the critic who counts, not the man who points out how the strong man stumbled, or where the doer of deeds could have done better. The credit belongs to the man who is actually in the arena.

— THEODORE ROOSEVELT

NORMAN VINCENT PEALE lived well into his nineties. One day someone commented that he had outlived his critics, and the answer came back, "No, he outloved them." Critics are very uncomfortable with love. It is hard to be critical of something you love, because love is blind to faults.

Imagine having to be a critic your entire life. Some people choose it as an occupation and some as an avocation. How can you enjoy what you are critical of? The answer is, you can't.

I am not talking about educating another person; I am talking about telling them what is wrong with them. I see it destroying relationships and families and more. You are a burden when you are a critic even when you are trying to save someone's life. Being critical of people doesn't change them.

Soulution of the Day

Love your critics, and love those you are critical of, and you will enjoy your life more.

DEATH AND REBIRTH

*Without an understanding of myth
or religion, without an understanding of
the relationship between destruction and
creation, death and rebirth, the individual
suffers the mysteries of life as
meaningless mayhem alone.*

— MARION WOODMAN

DEATH IS A BEGINNING. It feeds the living. If nature did not exist in cycles, life would end. The death of life in the fall of the year provides nourishment for the birth of life we awaken to every spring.

The death of what is killing us can bring us life, whether it is physical or emotional. I do not recommend killing people or other living things, but there are things in your life, such as inappropriate rules, regulations, and expectations, to name a few, that need to die in order to give you life. Overpowering desires and demands from others can kill you spiritually.

If you die spiritually, you will want to die physically too. Unfortunately, your body will attempt to fulfill your desire. You must accept your divine origin and move on to rebirth yourself and let the untrue self die.

Soulution of the Day

Rebirth can be very therapeutic.

BEAUTY
AND THE BEAST

Love all God's creation,
the whole and every grain of sand in it.

— FATHER ZOSSIMA,
IN *THE BROTHERS KARAMAZOV*

WE ALL KNOW THAT BEAUTY is in the eye of the beholder. We are so involved with our physical appearance that we frequently do not see the beauty before us. Our pets never linger in front of the mirror, nor do they fear to show themselves if they are missing a part or are overweight. They accept themselves. We, as humans, often see not the beauty but the beast when we look in the mirror.

If you see yourself as a beast you will go on a path of self-destruction. The day you can look in the mirror and see beauty is the day you will begin to care for yourself. Just as your self-love makes you beautiful, so does your love of others convince them of their beauty.

Beauty is not about perfection. It is not about your physical features. Yes, they can make you attractive, but true beauty is not about appearance. It is about your spirit and your soul. When you reflect their essence, you will be radiant, and people will be dazzled by your true beauty.

Soulution of the Day

Adjust your eyes to see beyond the mirror and into the truth.

CHAIN
OF COMMAND

We must live together as brothers
or perish together as fools.

— MARTIN LUTHER KING JR.

THE PHRASE "we must live together" refers, in my mind, to all living and nonliving things. We are all links in a chain. There really is no one in command, unless it is the One. We are all dependent on each other for warmth, light, food, shelter, fuel, energy, and our survival. Everything is dependent on something else, and even the smallest thing removed will affect the total chain.

Today species become extinct and others survive, but that is because we have a built-in security link in the chain. It gives us room to err and still maintain the balance. It is like an alarm system in your home. If you pay attention to the alarm, you can save your life.

Hopefully we will pay attention as links in the chain are eliminated. If the chain gets too small it will strangle all living things, and if the chain of life is broken, we will have lost our connection to our anchor. To begin again and reconstruct the chain is possible. All it takes is a few million years. Do we really want to see that happen, and do our children have the time?

Soulution of the Day

Maintain the integrity of every link in the chain of life
and remember what John Sebastian says in his song "Link in a Chain":
"And we got to keep the chain together till the end of time."

GET INVOLVED

The grave's a fine and private place,
but none, I think, do there embrace.

— ANDREW MARVELL

YOU MAY DONATE FUNDS to support noble causes, but do you also get involved? Are you afraid if you get involved you will only end up with more problems and with more demands made on you? When you see someone causing another person pain or discomfort, do you hesitate to get involved?

Think about what C. S. Lewis wrote about not giving your heart to anyone, not even an animal, "so it will not be broken; it will become unbreakable, impenetrable, and irredeemable." That is why we need to get involved. If we do not, we die inside. It is sad that we only get involved in times of a disaster, be it the World Trade Center tragedy or a war. Then we donate money and blood and show compassion.

Yes, you can be hurt by your involvement. But as Tennyson wrote, "'Tis better to have loved and lost than never to have loved at all." If you never love, you never live. So get involved and make your life meaningful. You will live a longer, healthier life, but that is not the only reason to do it.

Soulution of the Day

Get involved. You don't want to miss the chance to
perform a good deed or share love with another living thing.

PRESCRIPTION #329

DO YOUR THING

Whatever you do, you need courage.
Whatever course you decide upon, there is
always someone to tell you that you are
wrong. There are always difficulties arising
that tempt you to believe your critics are
right. To map out a course of action and
follow it to an end requires some of the same
courage that a soldier needs.

— RALPH WALDO EMERSON

ONE OF OUR SONS RECENTLY SAID he was proud of me for having had the courage to speak about my beliefs as a physician when they were not accepted by the medical profession. Back then it was exciting, in a sense, to be on every famous talk show and have people argue with me about how crazy my beliefs were. But I was also angry and tired of defending my beliefs in a scientific way.

I wasn't smart enough yet to just tell stories and be patient. However, I told my son that the reason I could take the criticism was because every day I came home to a family that loved me. My parents, wife, and children all accepted me, no matter what I said or did. They gave me the strength to be myself, to respect myself and maintain my sense of humor and self-esteem in the face of adversity.

I did not have to give up my life to please others and gain their acceptance. I could go on being who I was because others loved and believed in me and gave me the strength and courage to believe in myself. Being different was not a problem when I could come home to love.

Soulution of the Day

Have courage and find people who will support you
when you stand up for your beliefs. Be willing to be there for them too.

RARE BUTTERFLY

Be grateful for whoever comes,
because each has been sent
as a guide from beyond.

— RUMI

ONE EVENING I WAS AT A MEETING of Compassionate Friends, a group consisting of parents whose children have died. A father came up to me and started to tell me about his deceased son who had loved butterflies.

The summer after his son's death, the father had been walking in the woods near his Connecticut home. A beautiful, enormous butterfly followed him wherever he went. It gave him a wonderful feeling, and he felt it was his son coming back to help him deal with his grief.

When the father got home, he looked through his son's books to find a picture of the butterfly. To his amazement he found that the species that had been his uplifting companion in the woods actually existed only in South America.

We never know where or when a comforting messenger may appear, and what form it will take.

Soulution of the Day

When you are walking through a forest of grief, watch for messengers.

WASTE OF TIME

*Life is what happens while
you're busy making other plans.*

— JOHN LENNON

YOU DO SOMETHING and it doesn't work out. You go somewhere and are disappointed when you get there. You get stuck in traffic. What a waste of time! Is it really?

When you spend time feeling irritated about what happened or are upset over a failure, then you are truly wasting time. If you are willing to ask what you can learn from the experience, the wasted time ends. Problems and failures become teachers that may reward you someday, perhaps even more than success.

Even hitting bottom is not a waste of time. When you fail, it hurts. But the best way to stir the ground and prepare it for sowing a new crop is by hitting bottom and really kicking up a fuss. Let your fear get you moving. Every experience is worthwhile if we learn from it.

Soulution of the Day

*Time is only wasted when you allow it to be.
It is your lifetime. Use it.*

PRESCRIPTION #332

SIMPLICITY

Beauty when unadorned
is adorned the most.

— ATHENAEUS

KISS, OR "KEEP IT SIMPLE, STUPID," is a wise slogan. Simplicity makes things visible to everyone and therefore enlightens all who are exposed to what is presented. A good teacher does not make things more complicated, but simplifies what she presents to her students. When they comprehend, she can then move on to more complex things, which now seem simple to her students because of what she has already taught them.

Life is simple when you understand its nature. The fact that we cannot understand everything that has preceded us does not make it complicated. If you want people to know you, do not cover yourself with things that disguise you and cover up your true essence.

Take the time to know yourself and your simple essence, and then display it. Your life will become much less complicated when people know the simple truth about you. You will be able to devote your energy to what you believe and not to creating an image of yourself that deceives.

Soulution of the Day

Keep the plot of your life simple.

GIFTS

A book is not a gift until it is read.

— ANONYMOUS

WHEN SOMEONE IN YOUR FAMILY has a problem, be it physical or emotional, and you know there are ways they could help themselves, what do you do? If they do not ask for your advice and you tell them what they should do anyway, you become a burden, and most often they will feel judged and controlled. This sets up the whole situation for failure. They will not see your advice as a gift and will want to see less of you.

When you bring them a book or information and tell them that it has helped you, it truly is a gift. Your act says you care about them. The resource has been provided, and it is up to them to use it or not. However, if they never open the book or make a call, you must accept that too.

The gift is that you care. Everyone needs someone who cares. If you become the disciplinarian you destroy your gift. They must have the desire and intention to use the information, to read the book, to change their lifestyle, or whatever is needed of them. If you become the criticizing teacher, parent, or spouse you are destroying the gift that you have offered.

Soulution of the Day

Give your love and compassion in the form of a gift,
but remember this line from Al-Anon's credo,
"Just for today I will refrain from improving anybody except myself."

PORTRAITS

We seem to have lost contact with the earlier, more profound functions of art, which have always had to do with personal and collective empowerment, personal growth, communion with this world, and the search for what lies beneath and above this world.

— PETER LONDON

I PAINT PORTRAITS, and it helps me lose track of time and to heal. They also teach me to see what was before me. So I have become an observer as well as a painter.

When the family and our pets got tired of posing, I put up a mirror and painted a portrait of myself. I painted a hidden man, with cap, mask, and gown covering me as if I were in the operating room. At that time I could not see what covering everything up was doing to me. I couldn't observe the truth about myself because it was too painful. The painting helped me by being there every day until I saw the truth.

I can't paint a person or an animal in any way other than what feels natural to me. What began as a formal painting of my wife in an evening gown ended up as one of her standing with her bicycle.

Soulution of the Day

Observe yourself as if you were painting a portrait of your life.

PRESCRIPTION #335

HAVE FAITH

*Know that what is impenetrable to us
really exists, manifesting itself as the highest
wisdom and the most radiant beauty.*

— ALBERT EINSTEIN

A FEW YEARS AGO I traveled by ship, as part of a tour, to see the Alaskan wilderness. During one of the day trips to view a glacier, a sudden snowstorm limited my visibility. I became separated from my guide and the group. When the squall ceased, I could see no one, and there was no response to my calls.

Alone on the cold barren mountainside, I began to fear for my life. Then I remembered what I tell everyone at workshops: "When you don't know what to do, say a prayer." I prayed for God to save me, but nothing happened.

As it grew dark I began to give up hope until I saw someone approaching. I waved and attracted his attention. It was an Eskimo returning from a seal hunt. He tucked me into his sled and brought me back to civilization and my group. I felt God had deserted me until I realized who had sent the Eskimo.

Soulution of the Day

*You never know how God will answer your prayers.
Have faith; the answer may even come in the form of an Eskimo.*

MEASURE ME

Nobody has ever measured,
even poets, how much the heart can hold.

— ZELDA FITZGERALD

HOW DO WE TAKE the measure of a person and know how big he or she really is? Is it from the tips of the toes to the top of the head? Or is it the waistline or head size? I do not think any of these simple measurements takes the true measure of a person into consideration.

I say, measure me by the size of my heart. Take your tape measure and go around my heart, and include all the things my heart is touched by, and you will know how large I truly am.

The actions you take that spring from your heart have a far greater effect than those that come only from the mind or body. Open your heart and allow it to guide you in your actions.

One can become famous for physical accomplishments, but only the accomplishments of the heart truly fulfill. When one heart touches another, we have hearts beating in unison with no fear of rejection. A heart filled with love is eternal and not measurable by our hand.

Soulution of the Day

Give of your heart without measure.

ANIMALS

*Animals are reliable, many full of love,
true in their affections, predictable
in their actions, grateful and loyal;
difficult standards for people to live up to.*

— ALFRED A. MONTAPERT

IT IS VERY COLD OUTSIDE TODAY. The ground is covered with snow, and yet as I look out, there are beautiful birds nibbling at my bird feeder. They are not complaining about the weather or whining about the wind-chill factor. They are just flying about in all their glory, dining on the food I have put out. People need to act more like animals, to accept what is and find the glory and beauty in it.

Many emails I receive begin with how awful the weather is and go on talking about all the changes one has to make because of the weather. I say, God bless the weather and the animals. Sure, they have accidents in the house, but they weren't supposed to be kept in houses. They are animals, so I forgive them.

Animals accept what is and make the best of it.

Soulution of the Day

Act like an animal!

GIVE WHAT YOU WANT

*You give but little when you give
of your possessions. It is when you give of
yourself that you truly give.*

— KAHLIL GIBRAN

WHEN I TALK ABOUT giving what you want yourself, I am not speaking about only giving what you are willing to give away or about things that you no longer want. I am literally speaking about giving away what you yourself desire. If you want nothing, then give nothing. If you want love, then give love.

What you give away freely will come back to you. When I act in a loving way toward someone I know, she or he will ultimately return my love. I must continue to give in order to receive. How you treat others will ultimately be how they treat you.

But if you measure what you give, you will have no guarantee on what will be returned to you. When you give what you want, without measuring how much or what is returned, you give a gift to yourself, and it will be followed by gifts from others. How do you feel about the people who love you, give you gifts and material things with no demands or attachments? They do not burden you with guilt or a repayment schedule, and so they receive your gift of thanks in return.

Soulution of the Day

Give what you wish to receive.

HORNS
AND HALOS

*It is human nature to think wisely
and act in an absurd fashion.*

— ANATOLE FRANCE

I TRY TO PRACTICE WHAT I PREACH, but being human I have occasional lapses. It can be helpful to keep your family supplied with key phrases to remind you when you are acting human and not walking your talk.

A family I know is under a great deal of stress due to the mother's cancer. One day her nine-year-old daughter announced, "I think I need a pair of earplugs." When her parents asked her why she needed them, she told them it was because of their loud voices. Now the daughter's words have become a symbol that calms and quiets the household.

In our home when I lose it, my wife doesn't stop to reason with me. No apologies, explanations, discussions, just this: "Your noise is upsetting the children." The children are the four cats and a dog that live with us. I laugh, and we get on with life. When our five real children lived at home, their expression was, "Dad, you're not in the operating room now."

A friend of mine said to me, "You have a halo, but it's held up by your horns." I love it! That is human nature, plain and simple, the angel and devil within us. And as Jung said, "If God is at the front door the devil is at the back door."

Soulution of the Day

*Give your family a key phrase they can repeat
to remind you to wear your halo.*

CONDOLENCES

And that while we live,
she will be remembered with deep affection.

— OLIVER WENDELL HOLMES

EVERYONE EXPERIENCES LOSS, but many do not seek help to unlock the feelings that go with it and get stored within them. To bury grief and not express it can be self-destructive. We send therapists out to schools when a student dies suddenly and tragically, but we do not send therapists to your home or the hospital when loss is experienced.

Wallowing in sorrow does not heal us either. Remembering the beauty of what we have lost may. We need to share our feelings, and remember the person lost and how their life was a gift to us. Tears are normal and necessary to cleanse our wounds. Humor is appropriate and healing, and the joy of past experiences should be recalled with your loved ones.

By going to the funeral or the home of those who have lost a loved one, you help ease their sorrow. Each of us can take some of the pain home and help those mourning to heal. We cannot remove it all, but we can diminish it with our presence. By using what we have learned from the pain of our losses, we can ease the pain of those who are living with theirs.

Soulution of the Day

Embrace your grief and share your condolences;
it will help to heal everyone. Love is the only thing of permanence.

TEARS OF JOY

The most wasted of all days
is that on which one has not laughed.

— SEBASTIAN-ROCH
NICOLAS DE CHAMFORT

WHAT IS THE POINT OF LAUGHING? Laughter changes our body chemistry, makes us feel young again, and transforms relationships. It is very hard to be in conflict with someone who makes you laugh. They go from being your enemy to being a friend, even if you still question their sanity and behavior.

Why do tears become a part of laughter when the laughter is really uncontrolled? I think whether we laugh or cry, tears are a healing release and wash away our troubles. The more we store within us, and the less we react, the more harm we do to our bodies. Tears of any kind cleanse the soul.

Soulution of the Day

Cry your tears of joy and sorrow and help your body
to heal by eliminating the poisons that reside within.

PEACE OF MIND

*Remember, don't waste time comparing your
life to others who seem more fortunate.
Being fortunate is based on how much
peace you have, not how many luxuries or
conveniences you have. Practice from the
heart to make peace with what is.*

— DOC CHILDRE

AS I WRITE THIS, the holidays and the New Year are almost upon us. I am receiving greetings and cards from many people wishing me health, wealth, happiness, and good cheer. But I never read on that list of wishes the one thing I really want most: peace of mind.

I know people who have most of the things on the list, and they are all still unhappy. That is why I believe the most important thing to include is peace of mind, because without it, nothing will make us happy.

So when you send out your holiday greetings this year, remember to include the wish for peace of mind. May we all receive it this holiday season.

Soulution of the Day

Send out the message: Peace of Mind and Peace on Earth!

PRESCRIPTION #343

RETREAT FORWARD

*For centuries monasteries and convents
have opened their doors to men and women
who felt the need to withdraw from the
world and deepen their faith.*

— JOHN KORD LAGEMANN

SOMETIMES ONE MUST GO on a retreat in order to gain deeper insight into a situation and to develop possible solutions. The retreat does not have to be related to one's religion, but simply a way to help us gain insight into our journey and way of life. A retreat is not about running from the enemy but facing it and changing what we feel is threatening our desired joy.

You do not have to go far to retreat. You need to find a quiet place where you can feel free to question whatever you need to examine in your life, be it your religion, profession, relationships, or anything else that is important to you. A retreat may be a place to take a walk or work in a garden alone, a place that allows you to think, feel, and listen to your true inner voice.

Even by setting aside a place in your yard or home, you can have a retreat center to go to when you are in need of peace and clarity. The more you use your retreat, the greater the effect will be. A retreat allows you to tap your greater wisdom and reconnect with inner peace.

Soulution of the Day

Retreating to strengthen yourself is a step forward and an act of bravery.

RUNNING

I speak to you, be still.
Know I am God.

— ESSENE GOSPEL OF PEACE

Running to, running from,
Running away, running home,
Running until I find myself.
My heart pounds, I gasp for breath.
Running until I hear God's voice,
"You are home, you are safe, you are divine."
The running is over, my heart slows,
I breathe easily.

Soulution of the Day

Remember, the next time you are running, slow down and listen.
You are always home and safe in God's care.

DAWN

*Lift up your fallen spirits
for a new day soon will dawn.*

— NED NICOLS

THE SUN RISES, and the dawn of a new day presents itself — another chance to begin anew. Too often, however, we carry with us into the new day the problems of the past. We wish that we could go on sleeping rather than awaken.

When I feel like this, I step outside, and the peaceful beauty of nature surrounds me. I find gratitude replacing the burdens of my heart. I realize what is important to me. It is the small acts of kindness that sustain me, and the loving people in my life, not the worries, fears, lists, and schedules.

We all need to find a way to face each new day with gratitude and appreciation, to give thanks for the people and things in our lives, and to awaken to the dawn of a new day filled with joy and expectation.

Soulution of the Day

*Tomorrow when you wake up seek the beauty of the day
and leave the past behind. Be grateful.*

DISAGREEMENT

*We learn much from the disagreeable things
people say, for they make us think, whereas
the good things only make us glad.*

— THEODOR LESCHETIZKY

THERE ARE ONLY THREE THINGS in life that are certain: death, taxes and criticism. Criticism is often a difficult thing to deal with. But there is only one way to avoid it; if you do nothing and say nothing, no one can ever disagree with you.

When you have an honest opinion of yourself and your value as a person, you will be able to handle criticism. If you are going to survive disagreement and disagreeable people, you will need to find inner strength.

No one is liked by everyone. I can vouch for this, as can any public figure. Many will project their problems onto you, your words, or work. Be aware of the quality of your critic. Don't respond unless you know exactly what was said. It is always easier to be critical than correct.

The disagreements I always listen to come from those who love and care about me. Sometimes, before I defend myself, it helps me to find out what the reasons for the criticism were. It may change how I feel about the person once I am familiar with their wounds and problems. They are my teachers. I learn from them and think about what they have to say.

Soulution of the Day

Don't feel bad when someone criticizes you; it's one of the certainties of life.

LORD OF THE JUNGLE

Every man must live with the man he makes of himself.

— CARMINE BIRSAMATTO

WHAT DO YOU THINK ABOUT when you hear the term *lord of the jungle?* To me it implies an attitude of respect. Many animals must kill to live, but some still maintain a regal aura and sense of power about them that can intimidate and also command respect.

Could you be the lord of your jungle? How are you seen by the flock that shares the plains you live and work on? Do they fear your presence, or do they respect you for the protection you provide? Do they have the knowledge that you can be counted on to provide nourishment when it is needed?

It can take its toll on you to be the lord of the jungle, because there is stress involved in being a leader. Perhaps the secret is being in touch with and imitating the real Lord. When you do this, the stress will diminish because you will know who you truly work for.

Soulution of the Day

Who's the lord of your jungle?

RIGHT MOMENT

There is a tide in the affairs of men,
Which, taken at the flood,
leads on to fortune.

— **WILLIAM SHAKESPEARE,** *JULIUS CAESAR*

THERE IS A RIGHT MOMENT to act and speak. The same thing said at the wrong time can be a disaster, while spoken at the right time, enlightening. When we are angry we have to express it appropriately and at the right time. If not, the words that would have led to an improvement may make the situation worse.

So be aware of the appropriate timing and your emotional state before speaking. Also, while you are deciding on the right time or moment, be patient and aware of what others need. Sometimes the right moment for you is not right for the person you want to communicate with.

Timing is everything. If someone is homeless and without warm clothing for the winter ahead, donating your old winter clothes and food to the shelter the following spring is not very helpful. So think of what you can do when it makes the most difference. Your sense of timing and choice of action affect us all.

Soulution of the Day

As the Bible tells us, "To everything there is a season,
and a time to every purpose under heaven."

AMNESIA

Faults are thick where love is thin.

— ENGLISH PROVERB

AS I MENTIONED EARLIER, several years ago I fell off our roof when a wooden ladder broke as I put my weight on the top rung. I fell to the pavement, hitting my head on the driveway. I awakened to an attractive woman shaking me and asking, "Are you all right, honey?" I asked her why she kept calling me honey, and she said, "Because I'm your wife." From the blow to my head I had developed amnesia.

It improved my marriage and my relationship with our children dramatically. I couldn't remember anything that bothered me from the past or even the day before. We all got along wonderfully, until my memory began to return. Then I needed counseling.

The counselor said, "I'm going to save you time and money. Instead of coming for therapy for months, read this and do what it says." She handed me a slip of paper and I read it and have been trying to live up to its wisdom ever since. What she handed me was Corinthians 1:13: "Love is long suffering, love is kind, it is not jealous, love does not boast, it is not inflated. It is not discourteous, it is not selfish, it is not irritable, it does not enumerate the evil. It does not rejoice over the wrong, but rejoices in the truth. It covers all things, it has faith for all things, it hopes in all things, it endures in all things."

Love is blind to faults, so in that way it is as good as amnesia. But it also has many more advantages. It has helped me in all aspects of my life.

Soulution of the Day

If you can't bring yourself to love, then try amnesia until you are able to love.

CHALLENGE

That which we are, we are,
and if we are ever to be any better,
now is the time to begin.

— ALFRED, LORD TENNYSON

THE KEY IS to view change not as a threat but as a challenge and not to live in fear of the people or things that challenge us. To live in fear is to stop living and never to venture forth. Reprogram your brain and stop telling it that life is to be feared. Let it know that life is a challenge and you are ready to step forward and meet it.

Are you willing to take on the challenge and change your behavior and life, or is it easier for you to submit than be challenged? How long can you sit in your recliner with someone jabbing you with sharp, pointed objects before you respond? How much abuse are you willing to take? How long can someone or something continue to provoke you before you get up and do something? What will it take for you to rise to the challenge of making a change?

So respond to the challenges in your life. You cannot fail when you are representing your true self.

Soulution of the Day

Do the cha cha — challenge and change!

PRESCRIPTION #351

TREADING WATER

*Get beyond treading water and
day-to-day survival; live your life
with purpose.*

— Anonymous

The only reason I can see to tread water is if you fell off a boat and somebody was coming to rescue you. Even then, it would make sense to swim toward the boat and be rescued sooner. Treading water is like sitting and waiting with no sense of vitality or goal in mind.

There are times when I am waiting and it feels appropriate, at the moment, to just sit there and tread water. But it is more likely I will do something rather than just sit there. I want to be moving forward and doing something meaningful.

Do you have goals? Do you know where your life is headed? Or are you treading water until the current moves you along? If so, take some swimming lessons and get moving. Just keeping your head above water is not what life is about. In times of a disaster it may be what keeps you alive, but when life settles back down, get moving. I don't care what stroke you use. This is your life, so freestyle, breaststroke, or backstroke are fine. If you want to go unnoticed, take a deep breath and swim beneath the surface. Who cares what you use, as long as you get to the place you want to come ashore and plant your feet on solid ground.

Soulution of the Day

*Don't wait. Start swimming now.
Get your arms and legs moving toward your goals.*

TOGETHER

*Snowflakes are one of nature's
most fragile things, but just look what
they can do when they stick together.*

— VESTA M. KELLY

THE OTHER DAY I was listening to a song about togetherness. One line spoke about teaching and learning from each other. When two people do this they create a bond of togetherness because they are becoming one. When one permanently assumes the role of teacher and the other that of ignorant student, togetherness will not develop. But if you both keep changing places you will become united.

The Talmud tells us that when love is strong, a man and a woman can make their bed on a sword's blade. When love grows weak, a bed of sixty cubits is not large enough. For a couple to remain together through the difficult times, they must love and be attuned to each other.

In true love you are a team, a relationship, an entity — call it what you will. When you are together, you don't need words to tell you the meaning of togetherness. You feel it and you know how painful it is to be separated.

Soulution of the Day

Togetherness is a marriage of two souls with no need for a contract.

PRESCRIPTION #353

PRINCIPLES

*First decide what you want to do,
and then have the courage to start toward
the goal, no matter how impossible it looks.*

— HENRY KAISER

WE ALL LIVE BY PRINCIPLES. Some of us live by destructive ones
and others by productive and successful ones. In medicine no one
has studied the principles of success. When patients get well when
they aren't supposed to we call their recovery "spontaneous remis-
sions." What if we considered them cases of self-induced healing
and asked, "How did you do that?"

We also need to study the principles by which the successful
live, be it in healthcare, the business world, or just daily living.
When I read about successful people the same advice always seems
to be given: be persistent, find assistance, define your dream and
follow it, be sure it is meaningful for you and others, and live with
a sense of limited time.

When you follow these survival and success principles you will
see your life expand and grow. I want to emphasize being persistent.
If you believe in yourself you will not take no for an answer. You
will drive people crazy until they help you just to get you off their
backs. When they see the benefits of what you accomplish, they will
become your supporters.

Soulution of the Day

If you want to get ahead, learn from the principles of those who have.

WHERE THE BRAVE DARE NOT GO

*People who act in spite of their fear
are truly brave.*

— JAMES A. LaFOND-LEWIS

THERE IS NOWHERE the brave dare not go when the life of someone they love is being threatened. Wouldn't you rescue a loved one no matter what the risk? There are no limits to what the truly brave dare to do.

I watched a mother cat walk into a raging inferno to bring out her beloved kittens. She was burned and scarred but returned to the fire time after time until they were all rescued. Then she licked them and comforted them while ignoring her own wounds. She did this because she acted out of love and felt no pain until her acts of love were completed.

So it is with the brave. They take the challenge and transcend the physical and act out of love or for a noble cause. Time and body do not exist for the truly brave when they dare to do what others fear. But to run where the brave dare not go requires that true love be the reason for your actions.

Soulution of the Day

Love overcomes all fear, and we are all brave when we act out of love.

SMALL PLEASURES

Life is made up of small pleasures.
Happiness is made up of those tiny successes.
The big ones come too infrequently.
And if you don't collect all these tiny successes,
the big ones don't really mean anything.

— NORMAN LEAR

THERE ARE NO SMALL PLEASURES from my perspective, just as there is no small stuff to sweat. This is my life. It is all big stuff and great pleasures. I don't grade levels of pleasure; I just appreciate the moment and treasure the pleasure.

We are now grading pain, on a scale from one to ten, to help treat patients. That is because nurses and doctors can't know what you are feeling, and if they treat what they think you are experiencing, the treatment may be inadequate or too much at times. So they ask you what level your pain is at and then respond.

I cannot do that with pleasures. I can't say, "That was a ten" or "that was a two." Yes, I laugh harder at some jokes than others, but I am grateful for every smile and laugh, so they are all tens for me. When you appreciate life, you will find many little pleasures before you. Nature is made that way.

Soulution of the Day

Tomorrow make believe that this is your first day on earth
and enjoy the pleasures you never noticed as a long-time resident.

GOD'S WAY OF REMAINING ANONYMOUS

It's faith that really takes the courage,
the belief in things unseen.

— JACQUELYN MITCHARD

MANY TIMES I HAVE QUESTIONED a so-called coincidence that has occurred in my life. We talk about being led in a certain direction or finding our path or the reason events happen in our lives. Sometimes what appears to be a "bad break" or a disappointing circumstance turns out to be beneficial and leads us in a new and better direction.

When I was in Pittsburgh for my training in pediatric surgery, I developed severe pain and swelling in the joints of my fingers. I was diagnosed with arthritis. It was very difficult to operate, and I feared all my training was now without purpose.

At the same time, I was turned down for active military duty. The army did not want a disabled surgeon. Since that pathway was blocked for me, I returned to Connecticut. Very quickly the pain and swelling disappeared, and I saw the disease as a gift that had redirected me away from active military service. I continued with my training and with my chosen career path, which led me to become who I am today.

Soulution of the Day

Remember, sometimes what seems to be a negative incident
may well be an anonymous visitation from a Higher Power.

PRESCRIPTION #357

DIVINITY

We are Divine enough to ask and we are important enough to receive.

— **WAYNE DYER**

I BELIEVE WE ARE ALL of the same origin, and if we originate from the divine then we cannot deny that all is divine. Divine guidance is available to us all as well. But most of us tend to stop listening or put a block up to that guidance as soon as we become old enough to decide things for ourselves. We take detours and deviate from the path we were intended to follow. Eventually we all end up back in the divine, no matter what course we take, for it is the alpha and the omega. The ideal would be for us to view and live our entire journey as a divine experience.

When you reside in the divine, you are tranquil and free of fear. You are like the little child who has faith in her parents and knows she will be respected and loved. To live in the divine is to be held in the palm of God's hand. When I ask people to draw a picture of how they see their medical treatment, many draw themselves sitting or held in God's hand. They are more likely to survive than those who draw themselves going through hell.

I see myself as divine but accept the fact that I am not God. But I do know that I am connected to God and made of the same stuff. I am like the wire connected to the battery, and the current that runs through me is of divine origin.

Soulution of the Day

Accept and embrace your divinity and be lifted and guided by its energy.

WISH UPON
A STAR

*You are never given a wish without also
being given the power to make it true.
You may have to work for it, however.*

— RICHARD BACH

ONE OF MY FAVORITE SONGS speaks of wishing upon a star. It tells us that it does not matter who you are, you will still obtain your heart's desire. I know that when our hearts are one with our dreams, nothing is impossible. As the song says, "Everything your heart desires will come to you."

What would be the purpose of dreaming, if dreams never came true? They are not fantasy; they are the goals we need to reach out for. I am talking of the dreams of the heart of which the song lyrics speak. If your heart is in your dreams, you cannot be dreaming the wrong dreams, and you will have the power to make them come true.

Soulution of the Day

Never stop dreaming the dreams of your heart's desires.

JOYFULNESS

*The greatest gift you can give yourself is joy,
not only because of the feeling that goes
with it at the moment, but because of the
magnificent experience it will draw to you.
It will produce wonders in your life.*

— JACK BOLAND

HOW MUCH TIME do you spend a day visualizing joy? Everything you do affects your well-being, so why not choose to be joyful? We tend to spend more time visualizing and reliving past unpleasantries and those we expect in the future.

I certainly enjoy people and behaving like a joyful child when I am with them. But I'll bet I laugh more and experience more joy with our pets, who are just being their true selves and expressing their needs and desires. I, like our pets, choose joy, and it is because I refuse to spend my lifetime experiencing unpleasant feelings.

I don't deny that which is unpleasant, but I do not give my life to it. I deal with it, I respond to it, and then I move on to seek joy. It is not wrong to be joyful even in the midst of life's difficulties. To survive this life, find what brings you joy.

Soulution of the Day

*Seek joy. Bring it forth in your life and in the lives
of the people around you.*

MESSAGES

From listening comes wisdom.

— ITALIAN PROVERB

I OFTEN RECEIVE MESSAGES when I am out alone exercising. I think when I am doing a repetitive exercise like running or biking, I get into a trance state and I am more receptive. The messages are not coming from any one person, but from people I have known who have died or from the great field of conscious wisdom that exists for us all to tap into and learn from.

I have heard good-byes from people I know who have died, and the message is confirmed when I get home and the person's family calls to tell me of the death. I have been told what to say in lectures and at times of family crisis. I am amazed at the healing that takes place by the words I have been told to say or the questions I have been directed to ask.

It may be comfortable for you to reject this idea of messages, but I would advise you to stop and give yourself time to listen when they are being delivered.

Soulution of the Day

Do not be afraid to listen on all levels to all sources.

LOOK OUT

Sorrow looks back, worry looks around,
faith looks up.

— ANONYMOUS

WHEN DANGER APPROACHES everyone yells, "Look out." For what? That, they don't tell you. More often than not, you get into more trouble because you tense up and don't know what to protect yourself from. Most of the time what you are told to look out for never happens and is just coming from the fears and worries of other people.

You can look back and be sorry for what happened, what you did, and on and on. What good does looking back do? If you said you could learn from the past, I'd say fine, but now turn around and look ahead to accomplish something.

To truly look out means to open your eyes. Don't look in at your worries and sorrows; look out at the world before you. See the possibilities and have faith so you can raise your chin and look up. Elderly and disabled people, when sitting so that their chins drop and they can only look down, become depressed. Where you choose to look creates your destination.

Soulution of the Day

Look up, no matter what lies before you, if you want to overcome.

SURPRISES

*Even if it is a garden you know by heart
there are twelve months in the year
and every month means a different garden,
and the discovery of things unexpected
all the rest of the year.*

— MARGERY FISH

ON MY DESK sits a calendar with the statement for the day, "No matter how thin you slice it, there are always two sides." We are all unique and full of surprises. Life is not a bowl of cherries, but a basket of fruit. Who knows what will come next and who you will be from one day to the next. We need to live with a sense of surprise and be aware of the uniqueness of each day and not be surprised by that.

I always call myself a multiple personality, but I am still surprised, at times, by who shows up. Usually whoever shows up is fun, though there are times I have to make apologies for his behavior. The problem is our minds and how they handle surprises. Surprises and unexpected occurrences are all a part of life. You are not in charge, so sit back and enjoy.

Soulution of the Day

*If you are a multiple personality, like most of us,
someone in there knows how to handle the next surprise you encounter.*

WARMTH WITHIN

In the depth of winter I finally learned that there was in me an invincible summer.

— ALBERT CAMUS

WHY DO WE NEED WINTERTIME? Why would a Creator create short, cold days? I think it is because there are times we need to go within and be in touch with our inner source of energy and fire. What keeps us going during difficult times? What keeps us warm?

When we realize the message of winter, then how we perceive it changes. It is a time for coming together so we can warm each other. It is also a time to appreciate the beauty of white snow, the purity and beauty of whiteness, the blank canvas made by our Creator to remind us of the potential lying quietly beneath the surface waiting to come forth in time.

Winter teaches us an important life lesson: how to go inside and find what warms us under all conditions. So accept the chill and define what warms and energizes you and make it a part of your life. You will learn to survive the cold winters when all of life must struggle to survive, find food, and keep warm.

Life is a circle. Seasons come and go and the cycle continues, and so with our lives. Yes, someday our life will end, but just like a leaf we return to the love that made us, and we will nurture the life to come.

Soulution of the Day

Go inside yourself and ask what generates your heat and energy and allows you to survive and thrive in the darkest moments of your life.

NEW YEAR'S RESOLUTIONS

I don't want to make any resolutions.
I want to keep my old regrets.

— LUCY, FROM *PEANUTS*

IT IS NOT A BAD THING to make a New Year's resolution, but you can also continuously set yourself up to fail. Be realistic and forgiving. The best resolution is to accept your limitations and start from there. Resolve not to give up on yourself, and to love yourself, even when you don't like your behavior.

It is, as Lucy says, far easier to live with the old regrets and problems than to change. So resolve to practice doing what you have resolved, rather than achieving sainthood tomorrow.

As you write down your resolutions, remember these things: Be kind; do not set yourself up for failure by creating multiple resolutions that involve too much self-denial. Keep your goals manageable and realistic. The best resolutions leave one day of the week to enjoy being human and not living by any rules or expectations you have created.

Soulution of the Day

Resolve slowly so you don't get dizzy and fall down on the job.

PRESCRIPTION #365

NEW YEAR

We will open the book. Its pages are blank.
We are going to put words on them ourselves.
The book is called "Opportunity" and
its first chapter is New Year's Day.

— EDITH LOVEJOY PIERCE

A "NEW YEAR" — I think the term is an oxymoron. How can you have a new year? You are the same person, and the world doesn't start again with a clean slate. Your troubles don't disappear. People don't forgive you for what you did the year before. Unless you have amnesia, your life is anything but new when you awaken on the first day of the year. It is simply a way of measuring the passage of time. Why make such a fuss over it?

The truth lies in our desire to be reborn, to start again, to make resolutions and changes we can live up to. Then why wait for a certain date to start a new year? Why can't tomorrow be New Year's Day? Maybe it is!

I see it every day in my role as a physician; people learn they have a limited time to live, and they start their New Year behavior. They move, change jobs, spend more time with those they love, stop worrying about what everyone else thinks of them, and start to celebrate their life. They are grateful for the time they have to enjoy life and they stop whining about what they wish had happened during the past year.

When every evening is New Year's Eve and every day you awaken is New Year's Day, you are living life as it was intended.

Soulution of the Day

Tonight celebrate New Year's Eve and at midnight start to live your
New Year. But remember to celebrate the next night
and all that follows as well.

About the Author

D r. Bernie Siegel is a well-known proponent of alternative approaches to healing that heal not just the body, but the mind and soul as well. Bernie, as his friends and patients call him, studied medicine at Colgate University and Cornell University Medical College. His surgical training took place at Yale New Haven Hospital, West Haven Veteran's Hospital, and the Children's Hospital of Pittsburgh. In 1978 Bernie pioneered a new approach to group and individual cancer therapy called ECaP (Exceptional Cancer Patients). His innovative methods used patients' drawings, dreams, and feelings, and broke new ground in facilitating important lifestyle changes while engaging patients in the healing process. Bernie retired from general and pediatric surgical practice in 1989.

Always a strong advocate for his patients, Bernie has since dedicated himself to humanizing the medical establishment's approach to patients and empowering individuals to play a greater role in the healing process. He is an active speaker, traveling around the world to address patient and caregiver groups. As the author of several books, including *Love, Medicine & Miracles; Peace,*

Love & Healing; How to Live Between Office Visits; and *Prescriptions for Living,* Bernie has been at the forefront of the medical ethics and spiritual issues of our day. He and his wife (and occasional co-author), Bobbie, live in a suburb in Connecticut. They have five children and eight grandchildren.

New World Library is dedicated to
publishing books and audio projects
that inspire and challenge us to improve the quality
of our lives and our world.

Our books and audios are available
in bookstores everywhere.
For a catalog of our complete library
of fine books and audios, contact:

New World Library
14 Pamaron Way
Novato, CA 94949

Phone: (415) 884-2100
Fax: (415) 884-2199
Or call toll free (800) 972-6657
Catalog Requests: Ext. 50
Orders: Ext. 52

Email: escort@newworldlibrary.com
Website: www.newworldlibrary.com